FAT CHANCE

Fat Chance

SIMON GRAY

faber and faber
LONDON · BOSTON

First published in Great Britain in 1995
by Faber and Faber Limited
3 Queen Square London WC1N 3AU

Typeset by Faber and Faber Ltd
Printed in England by Clays Ltd, St Ives plc

© Simon Gray, 1995

Simon Gray is hereby identified as author of this
work in accordance with Section 77 of the Copyright,
Designs and Patents Act 1988

A CIP record for this book
is available from the British Library

ISBN 0–571–17792–1

2 4 6 8 10 9 7 5 3 1

For Rik

PART I

This morning I woke to discover that both pairs of swimming trunks, my new ones, had been stolen from the porch, along with the duty-free cigarettes and lighter. Also my watch has stopped, and refuses to start, whether caressed or beaten. The wind is howling, the rain torrential. So the hell with it. Let's go for some memories. Memories of *Cell Mates*.

Every night when we went through the stage door at Guildford or Richmond or the Albery in London, there were the Rik Mayall groupies waiting with their autograph books and their cameras — girls and boys, more girls than boys, to pay their tributes, give him their homage and love. He treated them with lively openness, joking with them as he signed and posed for them, never patronizing or posturing. The Stephen Fry groupies were older and more dignified, standing shyly to the side but with their programmes extended, their pens in their hands. Stephen received them with the manners of a convivial prelate.

During a short break in rehearsals Stephen launched into a story, a true story, he'd come across about penguins. Kind of rogue penguins, really, or perhaps sybaritic penguins, as they'd settled on a beach in a soft, warm country and stayed there, instead of going to their icy offices in freezing climates. Anyway, they had become a great tourist attraction; and even had a kind of official compere figure, to introduce the tourists to the penguins, and vice versa. The tourists would assemble at, say, 4 p.m. and stare eagerly towards a blank sea, as the compere filled them in on the nature and habits of penguins generally, and of these sun-loving 'sports' in particular. Occasionally, he'd interrupt himself with, 'Don't worry, they'll be here in three minutes' – then, 'one minute, don't worry' – then, 'ten seconds'. Still only a blank sea for the next ten seconds, when, on the dot, a solitary penguin suddenly emerged from the sea on to the beach, looked around as if clocking the house, looked back towards the sea with a kind of bow, summoning on to the beach the rest of his company. They walked through the ranks of camera-aiming tourists, giving occasional bows and nods, and even going back, Stephen swore, if they felt one or other of the tourists had fudged the photograph. Stephen told us all this with such charm and wit and fluency that he filled the rehearsal room with affectionate laughter.

One evening after a preview of *Cell Mates* at Richmond, absolutely exhausted, I enquired back-stage if there was any chance of getting a lift to Holland Park. Stephen said at once, ever generous, that I could come in his taxi, if I didn't mind waiting while he talked to his friends (Ben Elton and wife) for a while. I said I'd go to the pub for a drink – perhaps he'd like to join me. Better not have a drink, Stephen said, because of the taxi and everything. I went to the pub, not really puzzling over why a chap travelling in a taxi couldn't have a drink – one of the main points about taxis is that you *can* have a drink. I sat brooding about my play and my production of it, until Rik appeared to fetch me. He downed a quick Scotch, we went back to the stage door, where Stephen and the Eltons were chatting beside the taxi. 'Well, let's go,' Stephen said, courteously opening the door and ushering us in. 'But where's the bloody driver?' I said, with my usual grace. The bloody driver, in the form and shape of Stephen himself, clambered into the driving seat and drove us back to London, with great skill too – employing all the manoeuvrability of the London cab. It was one of the most enchanting little trips of my life – the Eltons, Rik and I spontaneously interrupting our conversation to laugh in a kind of pleased disbelief at our situation; occasionally dishing out orders to our cabbie, whose bulk and own laughter doubled the sense of festivity. I mean, what can one do but adore (and be touched by, curiously) a man who owns and drives his own taxi, in the service of his friends. And has the wherewithal to do it. That evening anyway, God was in His heaven, and all was right with the world. Or perhaps God wasn't in His heaven, which was why all was right with the world.

Other rides in other taxis. Rik's habit of stopping at the off-licence nearest to the Old Vic rehearsal rooms to pick up a can of beer, his enjoyment at being recognized by the Pakistani chap at the counter, his sipping the beer down in the taxi, Stephen's flow of anecdotes, Rik suddenly subsiding into bouts of rumination. Then Rik lighting up a cigarette, lighting up Stephen's cigarette, lighting up mine. Once I pointed out the 'Thank you for not smoking' sign. Rik said, 'Don't worry. I'm Rik Mayall. I can do anything I like.' And the taxi drivers did let him do what he liked – drink beer, smoke cigarettes as he ruminated away, while from Stephen the anecdotes, analyses and artistic allusions flowed and flowed.

The occasion when Rik and I had just dropped Stephen off at his flat in Piccadilly. As we crawled through the traffic along the Old Brompton Road, Rik, in response to some casual – anyway, it certainly wasn't probing – question of mine about his evident delight in acting, where did he think it came from? that sort of thing, went into an intense, introspective monologue. The burden of it was that he could get through life only by pretending to be other people. He ended with an abruptly fatalistic declaration that sometimes in private – even completely in private and on his own – he seemed to be pretending to be Rik Mayall. I couldn't help wondering who Rik Mayall was pretending to be when telling me about only pretending to be Rik Mayall. When I glanced at him from time to time during the rest of the journey – he always sat absolutely upright, a can of lager in his hand, on the fold-up seat across from me – he was staring straight ahead, smiling his famous Rik Mayall smile. Actually, there was something oddly bewildered about both the stare and the smile, as if for once he'd been ambushed by confusion and was meeting it with an automatic attempt at performance, without knowing quite what to perform. When we got to the bar at the Halcyon, he simply turned into a chap who was desperate for a pee. No pretence about that. And no pretension or pretence in the worried, determined way in which he rehearsed the day's rehearsal, questioning, questioning, questioning. When it came to his work, Rik was uninhibitedly *au naturel*.

I seemed always to have terrible trouble in getting anywhere that I had to be for the production. Even the simple twenty-minute cab journey from w11 to Waterloo, for rehearsals at the Old Vic, were complicated, distorted even, by preposterous circumstances – one trip taking an hour and a half because of rain and the closing down of one of the bridges across the Thames, another taking almost as long because of a mass demonstration for or against something or other (all I can remember of this, as we sat stagnantly on the road, was having to repress an infuriated impulse to get out and demonstrate against the demonstrators). And then there was the taxi that failed to turn up because the dispatcher had booked it in for the following day – on what grounds, I can't imagine, as I'd done the usual thing, which was simply to phone up and ask for a (smoking) taxi immediately. Getting to Guildford, which also involved a taxi to Waterloo, was even worse. It should have been a thirty-minute journey on the train from Waterloo station to Guildford station, and then a five-minute taxi ride to the Yvonne Arnaud Theatre. I was twice misdirected by British Rail officials to the wrong platform, and boarded a train that stopped at what seemed like fifteen or so stations before Guildford. And there was the train that simply stopped because it felt ill or tired or something. And then there was the derailment at Waterloo, announced a moment after I'd bought my ticket, which resulted in my cabbing to Clapham Junction and waiting in the rain for a train that, though mentioned now and then on the loud-speakers, never turned up. And so it went and so it went, and so I didn't go anywhere with normal ease and confidence, not even to Richmond, the roads to which were invariably blocked by fire engines, slewed trucks and so forth. I was never very late, owing to my habit of leaving very early, but I became increasingly tormented by the sense of being jinxed. Or of the production being jinxed. No, I never thought *that*, actually, although I should have done. I just assumed I was in a private conflict with the gods of travel.

Stephen, on the other hand, was twice seriously late for rehearsals – something generally unacceptable in the theatre, where such considerations as punctuality are taken in an almost military spirit. On both occasions he'd had very late nights, followed by rather early mornings (one involving breakfast at the Ritz or Savoy), followed by something or other either social or to do with one of his many other careers, followed by a trip home to collect himself (and his script, I presume), followed by a brief nap, followed by a long, unintended and very deep sleep. He arrived an hour and a half overdue, during which time I'd gone a hideous journey, from irritation to anger to rage to outrage to worry to extreme agitation to despair. I suspect from my memories of Rik's expression that he was going down the same emotional passages. We certainly ended up blankly, hopelessly asserting that something had 'happened', something dreadful must have 'happened' to him. Like parents of adolescents, in fact, at four in the morning. When he finally turned up, shortly after the stage management had left to find him – to knock down his front door, if necessary – we were so relieved to see him, Rik and I, so joyously relieved, that instead of giving him the sound tongue-lashing, not to say flogging, his behaviour deserved, we actually celebrated his appearance with cries of relief and forgiveness. And he was so charmingly humble and ashamed, so continuously apologetic. Now, of course, I tend to interpret this incident as a symptom. Was this brief, stressful absence a dry-run at the comprehensively distressing absence that was to come? An unconscious rehearsal for a conscious act of defection? But everything falls into place when considered backwards. Possibly into the wrong place. So let's leave it that he merely fell asleep when he shouldn't have.

Well into rehearsals at the Old Vic, as we were getting into the lift at the end of a day's work, Stephen said that he'd never, ever in his life, enjoyed rehearsals as much. Not for theatre, not for film, not for television – it was 'sheer joy. Bliss'. Rik agreed, with a characteristic combination of cheerfulness and torment. I'd have agreed, too, if I hadn't been in the grip of an almost perpetual nervous dread that went every morning straight to my stomach and clutched there like a crab's claws. But there's no doubt that they were exceptionally harmonious and cheerful and delightfully concentrated hours, those hours of those days at the Old Vic – the concentration alleviated by short breaks in which Stephen and Rik romped with each other like toddlers, making up stories, fantasies, dirty jokes, going on surreal flights together – but Rik would suddenly exit from this delirium to focus on me with a confusingly expressed question that had at its heart an alert anxiety. I'd do my best to deal with this, and then off they'd go again, gambolling in their pleasure of each other. Sometimes I found myself drawn in, as on one evening after rehearsal when the three of us elaborated on an impromptu idea of a theatre critic ascending to heaven, pad and pencil in his hand, taking notes as he went – 'my end too rapid, unexpected, dramatically completely unjustified' – taking further notes on arrival, jotting down unfavourable observations on the scenery – 'shapeless, formless, without definition' – the lighting – 'bright and vulgar, the music – 'all harps and no sharps' – until he got around to the Director Himself – 'bumbling and inept, saddled Himself with an enormous cast to no particular purpose'. It was a delirious half hour, the more so for coming out of nowhere, unplanned, sublimely silly.

The only time I felt uneasy, not to say downright queasy, was when the two of them would suddenly and ebulliently, almost jeeringly, do turns from *Macbeth*, Stephen reeling off long speeches, Rik shouting, 'Macbeth! That's from Macbeth!' I suppose it was their way of proclaiming that they came from a different world, a world without established theatrical traditions – in this case, the embedded one, deeply embedded one, of never quoting from or mentioning the title of the work that most actors refer to evasively, because it's always associated with bad luck, as 'the Scottish play'. I can't say I've ever within myself honoured that particular superstition, but I was sure that other actors in the rehearsal room did, and I felt that, whether you honour a superstition within yourself or not, it's always safer to honour other people's honouring of superstitions. Especially when the superstition might be the consequence of accumulated experience – to which can now be added, come to think of it, the experience of *Cell Mates* itself. But apart from this, the rollicking, the frolicking, the gambolling were sheer fun.

A conversation with Stephen over dinner in the Ivy. The subject was the traditional much-debated – possibly over-debated – opposition between evolution and religion. Stephen, a hard-line, even fervent evolutionist, suddenly got up and stumbled blankly out of the conversation, evidently deeply affronted by my soft-lined, not particularly fervent defence of religion as a metaphor for the need to answer the inexplicabilities of life and death. Next day before rehearsals I phoned him to find out if he was all right. He said how relieved he was that I hadn't taken offence at 'this ridiculous man gabbling out in anger'. He seemed to think that his behaviour had been noticed with derision and contempt by everyone in the restaurant, including the waiters. Which, of course, was not the case. He'd merely looked like a man having a passionately intellectual dispute over a dinner table. Or possibly, from the waiters' point of view, a passionate dispute over responsibility for the bill.

One lunch-time in Groucho's, after a recording session, it was Rik who terminated a conversation. For some reason, but I can't remember how or why, we found ourselves discussing, firstly sexual perversion in general, then paedophilia in particular. The one perversion, Rik said, he could neither understand nor bear the thought of. Stephen characteristically and eagerly entered into one of his slightly confusing philosophical/anthropological discourses – pederasty in ancient Greece kind of stuff, I suppose, though I wasn't listening very closely, being too aware of Rik (the father of two young children) becoming increasingly agitated. He got up abruptly, saying he wanted to walk back to rehearsals, over the bridge. Stephen, virtually in mid-sentence, looked completely baffled. We got a taxi to the Old Vic, thought

7

we saw Rik on Waterloo Bridge, trudging angrily across it. Ordered the driver to draw up beside him. Wasn't Rik. Rik was already at rehearsals, full of apologies for his dramatic departure. Stephen and I accepted them graciously, although I had an ashamed sense that the apologies were the wrong way round. (On the way into the rehearsal room, Stephen said he hated his body, wished he was just a brain, immobile. I said, truthfully, that I thought he had a perfectly charming body. He was surprised, quite excited, said, 'Really? Do you really think that? How sweet – how very sweet of you.')

I'm no good at all at orchestrating curtain calls, so at Guildford, before the first preview, I handed the job over to the production manager. He achieved a rather touching final effect that balanced the double act of Rik and Stephen with the ensemble work of the *Cell Mates* company – an effect fatally ruined by Rik's stepping not only out of character but out of the play and the production, curtsying again and again, then bum-wagging almost off stage before turning suddenly for a last dip, curtsy, a gleaming roll of the eyes. I endured this for several evenings, until I realized that unless I said something it would continue, so I decided – as they say – to 'say something'.

It was the only – and very gently conducted – altercation Rik and I have ever had. His position was that he had a lot of fans very special to himself out there, and they deserved his very special acknowledgement. That was the tradition (stand-up comic, music hall) he came from. My position was that I came from a staid theatrical tradition – the audience should be applauding the actor through the character, I said, and not a famous personality who seemed suddenly to have abandoned all contact with both the play and his own (very special) performance. We battled through this and came to the only reasonable agreement. That he would do as I said. And he did. And that was that. Although he finally won – game, set and match – when he was playing at the Albery, first with an understudy, then with Stephen's replacement, Simon Ward, by gesturing to them with such lavish generosity – I mean, I couldn't say, could I, cut

8

out all this eye-catching deference to others? Especially under the circumstances.

One evening I went into Guildford for a rehearsal, to find David Bownes, the company manager, in something more intense than his usual mood of warm and sensitive gloom. Stephen, he said, had received an anonymous letter of the kind that famous personalities inevitably get from time to time. Warning him that 'they', whoever 'they' were, were out to get him. So this was one of the prices Stephen Fry paid for Stephen Fry's fame. He went on stage that night, knowing that some loony, even a couple of loonies, might be waiting for him in the auditorium.

On the other hand, there was his lunch with one of the tabloids. The journalist, I don't know whether a man or a woman, came down to Stephen's very expensive hotel in Hazlemere, outside Guildford. They shared a lunch that cost the tabloid hundreds of pounds – the interviewer making the fatal mistake of asking Stephen to choose the wines. Stephen, knowing wines and habitually indifferent to their cost, chose from deep cellars and long ago. Now is this merely Stephen unable to resist a binge? Or is it Stephen, the serious critic of the press comically making a serious point – that what the press wants to know it has to pay for, and extravagantly? I have no idea – one day life-threatening obscenities in the post, followed another day by obscene and possibly life-threatening lunches.

The point about the murderous letter sent to Stephen, the extravagant tabloid lunch at the expensive hotel, is that Stephen seemed to be caught between two sorts of lives that were in a sense identical. Wined and lunched because he was a famous *personality*, physically threatened because he was a famous *personality* – and yet, in spite of the one, in spite of the other, at that stage anyway, nobly 'treading the boards' (in his own words, words I came to hate). There was a valour in it. He attempted to suppress his terror of the letter, he told anecdotes about his magnificently squandering lunch and, millionaire or not, famous or not, 'trod the boards'. At Guildford and Richmond, anyway. Quel homme!

*

Two last memories, of Guildford. One, at the party after the first preview, of Rik and his wife, Barbara. Barbara glowed in that almost mystical manner one associates with women newly pregnant, which, as it turned out, she was. Rik was in double shock – the shock of giving his first public performance in *Cell Mates*, which had been either immediately preceded by or immediately followed by the shock of discovering that he was shortly to be a father again. He sat beside Barbara as if he were also sitting at her feet.

The other Guildford memory. After the show one night I was having dinner in the theatre restaurant with Victoria, my companion in life, and Sarah, my assistant. Stephen, carrying bags of laundry, joined us. As he made a short meal from amply filled plates, he went into a light-hearted confession (*à propos* the laundry, I suppose) about his life-long need to appear grown up. He cited as a no-longer-valuable role model an Etonian he'd heard about who was in the habit of spinning off to London in the evening, then turning up the next morning still in last night's dinner jacket. He would loll at his desk and run an electric shaver over his chops, as he explained to his peers and to his teacher – who was clearly rendered by this act less than a peer – that he'd had a heavy night on the town but was anxious to look clean and bright for the lesson. Stephen's mimicry of a languid, Etonian socialite was – like his telling of the penguin story – full of charm and wit. It was also full of rueful envy. 'I wish I'd had the nerve to do that sort of thing,' he said, 'when I was that age. I wish I had the nerve to do it now.' After he'd finished eating, after further anecdotes, he left for his hotel, his luxurious solitude and some late-night work on a film script. Hurrying through the restaurant, he looked, with his convict hair-cut, his bags of laundry and his odd, endearing gait – somewhere between a lumber and a toddle – like a schoolboy himself. A large one, not Etonian, from more than fifty years ago.

A last memory from London. The first day of rehearsals at the Old Vic, after the read-through. Stephen and other members of the cast asked me if I was going to keep a production diary as I'd done on two previous occasions. I said that there were no circumstances – no circumstances! – absolutely no circumstances in which I would ever again write about a production of mine. So bang! goes Fate with his fist. Bang! Bang! Bang!

PART II

I don't know exactly where to begin the story of *Cell Mates*, unless at the beginning of the writing of it, which was some five years ago. I was in Tucson, Arizona, directing a revised (to the point of obliteration, I fear) play of mine. In the mornings, before rehearsal, I began making notes on a project commissioned by the BBC – the story of the relationship between George Blake and Sean Bourke. What follows is merely my understanding of the story. Anyway, it's the story I wanted to tell.

Blake and Bourke met each other in Wormwood Scrubs prison in the early 1960s. Bourke was doing time for sending a letter bomb to the detective inspector who'd 'set him up', according to Bourke's account, for corrupting young men at the youth centre in Brighton at which he was then working. This youth centre was, for Bourke, an Irishman with a long record of petty crime in Dublin and London, a chance for self-rehabilitation. The detective inspector's charges threatened to ruin his nearly stabilized life. Hence the letter bomb, on which he'd left fingerprints, and had wired incorrectly. So he was arrested, found guilty, sent down for seven years. Blake, on the other hand, was sentenced to forty-two years, the longest sentence ever dished out in Britain, for spying for the Russians. He reputedly sent forty-two Western spies (so presumably the sentence was a mathematically moral calculation) to their deaths by betraying their names from the Russian desk in his office at MI5. He was, or rather is (he's still alive as I write this), of Dutch-Egyptian descent, his Egyptian parentage on his father's side entitling him in those days to British citizenship. He was, at a tender age, a courier for the Dutch underground during the Nazi occupation until his

12

activities became known to the Nazis, whereupon his family persuaded him to flee to England. Here he spent a brief time in school, joined the submarine corps, found he was terrified by life under water, and moved into the Foreign Office. He knew Dutch, Arabic, had a great gift for languages (though not truly for English: in his self-justifying television appearances he's always sounded like an Afrikaner). In due course he was posted to South Korea. When it was overrun by the North Korean communists, he refused to depart though departure was available, stayed on to be captured, was compounded with American soldiers whose lives he attempted to save, strove to escape, was recaptured, subjected to brainwashing (as it was then called) and eventually got back to England, to a hero's welcome, and a move from the Foreign Office to the MI5 Russian desk. He himself has claimed in his autobiography that he wasn't converted to Marxism by the brainwashing in Korea, but by an English civil servant who did brisk, fair-minded courses on the principles of Marxism at Downing College in Cambridge. Through whatever means, whether the course at Cambridge or the brainwashing in Korea, Blake became an agent of the KGB. For him, the USSR was 'the country of the future' – the last line of the play.

They met up, these two men, both of the same sort of age, in Wormwood Scrubs. Bourke, the Irish renegade and petty criminal, who'd endured a childhood and adolescence of savage corrective beatings – his teachers were Jesuits – before turning to crime and drink as a form, I suppose, of rebellion, and the strictly self-disciplined Blake, a spy and traitor with the highest (as he saw it) of moral principles. They were both intelligent men, from very different backgrounds, who fell into an instinctive alliance. Or an alliance manipulated by Blake, who'd instinctively detected in Bourke a way out of Wormwood Scrubs. Bourke, the editor of the prison magazine, detected in Blake a master spirit, an educated man from a different world whose respect he coveted. I think Bourke loved Blake from the beginning. I also think Blake loved Bourke, but didn't have enough experience of the emotional life to acknowledge it – even though at the time of his arrest he was apparently happily married with children, while

Bourke, the habitué of pubs, the roistering, almost clichéd Irishman, spontaneous, gregarious, affectionate, had had no lasting relationships that one knows of. Bourke, with only a year or so to go in the Scrubs when he met Blake, promised to help spring him, the most important prisoner, the 'star' prisoner in the British Isles. He kept his promise. With the help of a walkie-talkie he had managed to smuggle to Blake, and then a rope ladder and a car hired under an assumed name, he got Blake out of the Scrubs and into a bed-sitter, just around the corner from the prison. A year later Bourke transported Blake to Moscow, hiding him behind a false door under a children's bunk, in a Dormobile owned and driven by a couple of anti-nuclear campaigners with whom both Bourke and Blake had made friends in the Scrubs. Before leaving, Blake had persuaded Bourke (who yearned to get back to Dublin, to tell his story in the pubs, in the newspapers, in a book, above all in a book) to follow him to Moscow – for a week or two, no more, as Bourke understood it – and then on to Dublin for Bourke. Blake managed by various stratagems to detain him in Moscow for two years. During this period, Blake was writing an official autobiography which the KGB thought would be a propaganda coup. He loathed doing it, finding the subject of himself, as he confessed in an autobiography completed years later, thoroughly boring, and was relieved that his account turned out to be unpublishable, even in Moscow. Bourke was simultaneously, but surreptitiously, writing his version of the manner in which he had engineered Blake's escape. This was eventually published as *The Springing of George Blake*.

Blake's need to keep Bourke in Moscow has never been adequately explained. There are two alternative, but not contradictory, possibilities. One, that Blake found it humiliating that his freedom – if freedom is what he had in Moscow – had been achieved by one man, 'a single Irish fella'. The KGB, his employers and beneficiaries, had made not the slightest effort to assist him from the moment of his arrest. By keeping Bourke in Moscow, Blake at least prevented Bourke from publishing the embarrassing truth. And two, that Blake depended on his liberator. After such dramatic and closeted experiences with him in the Scrubs and then in London in hiding with him, he couldn't bear the thought of life – especially a life in Moscow – without him.

Whichever alternative one plumps for – and in *Cell Mates* I plumped for both – it seems clear that Blake played on Bourke's terror of the KGB and his innate hatred/fear of authority to keep him penned in his flat. When Bourke kept insisting that he needed, desperately needed, to go home to Dublin, Blake told him that if he tried, the KGB would kill him. In fact, they were probably going to kill him anyway. A bad move, as Bourke, terrorized, went on the run. He hid out in the local woods – it was Moscow mid-winter, freezing – slept under newspapers, and ended up, after six weeks and without money or the Russian language, begging for food, a tramp. When he could endure no more, he returned to Blake's apartment. The two KGB officials in charge of their cases assured him that, if he truly wanted to go back to Dublin, then Dublin was where he should go, they themselves would make it possible to get him there. They were furious with Blake and humiliated him in front of Bourke, in a kind of tame, domestic show trial. They were decent men who felt that they and their department had been sullied by Blake's complicated conspiracy.

So Bourke finally made it back to Dublin, got himself into the newspapers, published his book, and became, for a time, the pub hero he'd always longed to be. He fought, successfully, the British government's attempts to extradite him to stand trial for his part in Blake's escape. This was his last, great moment. He told his story, the same story, again and again. There was no more in the way of a story to come. He turned into a famously to-be-avoided bore, dying either in a houseboat on a canal or on a pavement outside one of his favourite pubs where he was no longer favoured – there are various, though very few, versions of his death. *Cell Mates* doesn't follow Bourke to Dublin and his decline; it ends with his separation from Blake in Moscow.

The primary source material of the play was Bourke's *The Springing of George Blake*. Blake's autobiography devotes only three pages to the springing, the escape, the years spent with Bourke, his liberator. Those three pages, blandly patronizing in their treatment (dismissal, really) of Bourke, made me so contemptuous of Blake that I constantly choked when attempting to write the many drafts and versions of the film, the radio play, the screenplay. It took me, on and off, something like five years to get close to Blake, to tolerate and even to excuse him. It was only when I realized how lonely he must have been in his perpetual and self-imprisoning secretiveness that the story assumed a shape that worked. For me, anyway.

When I finally produced a film script that satisfied the BBC producer, the director of our choice and myself, I was invited to an interview with the head of one of the drama departments. He sat behind his desk, cool and correct, a combination of schoolmaster and Anglican minister. He said he liked the script a lot and so did his script editor. He nodded to his script editor, a pleasant-faced woman in her thirties, who struck me as someone out of the Workers' Revolutionary Party. She said she also liked it a lot, a lot more than most of my other work, yes, she liked it far, far better than almost anything that had appeared on the screen under my name, and she didn't really have any reservations. Not really. The head of the department then came rolling around the desk in his wheelchair – he had been the victim of a car accident some years back – and proclaimed that these days it didn't matter how good the script was, what they needed was stars, yes, stars – his voice reverberating on the word as if he were talking of Christs – stars to put bums on seats. The producer, an odd, vaguely ex-European (i.e. not British) chap with a lisp and rolling foreign 'r's, made a counter-peroration in agreement and disagreement – yes, he said, *of course* we needed a couple of stars, but on the other hand the story was so good that what we needed was serious actors who could do the parts, to hell with the stars, whom he agreed we needed. The pleasant-faced script editor chipped in with some blatantly capitalist affirmations of her boss's spiritually resonant position – 'Get us some stars,' she said, 'and we'll get the show on the screen.' We left, the producer, the director and I, with the head of drama

16

rolling back behind his desk, the script editor smiling placidly at the thought of another job done, another execution faultlessly executed.

The director and I talked from time to time, coming up with names of famous actors who, we believed, could do the parts. They were passed on to the producer, who took them in the form of memos to the overlord and his script editor, rather as certain domestic pets leave dead mice and birds outside their owner's door, to roughly, I suspect, the same reception – a sorrowfully disgusted shake of the head.

I gave up on the BBC, feeling that the BBC had given up on writers, and this one in particular, but I didn't, couldn't give up on Bourke and Blake. I wanted them, no, needed them, to live in some form, if not on screen, on stage perhaps. I set about rewriting, first following the line of the film script and then, as I burrowed further into it, becoming more and more involved with the two central characters. I suddenly found myself, in order to burrow some more, going in a quite different direction, turning the play into a weird duologue in which there were two voices but four characters, Blake, Bourke, and the two tape recorders they each spoke into as they wrote their respective books.

I sent it off to Michael Codron, the producer with whom I went back some thirty years. He responded quickly – which he always does, a great virtue in a producer – and enthusiastically, which delighted me, as enthusiasm is always a producer's greatest virtue. The play at that time was called, by the way, *Says I Says He*. I won't go into all the ins and outs of what followed, but here is – I hope – a swiftish summary. Two very famous (though not by the BBC's standards – one of them had been greeted as dead prey by the overlord and his script editor) actors, to whom I'd sent the play before I'd sent it to Michael, were both eager to do it, one going for Blake, the other for Bourke. I raised these names with Michael; he gave them his blessing, withdrew his blessing, interviewed them with me – we both knew them and their work very well – because he said he wanted to see what they looked like side by side, though as one was small, dark and famously handsome, the other a trifle portly, with gingery-white hair and a famously vibrant physique, we didn't actually have to see them seated, with elbows touching, to know what they'd look like side by side. So what was Michael really up to in organizing this unnecessary charade? My suspicion was that it expressed formally a growing uncertainty about the play itself. A suspicion that was confirmed when week by week he withdrew his blessings, first from one actor, then from the other, then from the play. He didn't actually excommunicate so much as dither, bow and procrastinate his way out of a situation that he'd clearly come to find embarrassing. I learned later that he'd taken advice from a couple of directors who'd pronounced the text undirectable. At least by them.

As a matter of fact, I thought they were right. They must have been because, before I'd received this news, I'd gone back to the drawing board – 'Ah well, back to the drawing board,' my late agent and still much-lamented friend, Clive Goodwin, had said on the occasion of a resounding flop of mine at the RSC – 'Ah well, back to the drawing board.' Which is where I was with the play that was to become *Cell Mates*. I sent it off to its next port of call, the producer Duncan Weldon, who some years ago produced a play of mine, *Melon*, with Alan Bates in the lead. Duncan has an extraordinary appetite for stars, most particularly American ones who have become world-famous through films, and has a gift, in spite of an innate social reticence – shyness, I suppose – for luring them on to the boards in London. In that respect he's a legend. So much so that when Alan, during his *Melon* days, was visited backstage by a director friend, Alan's complaint about never getting as much as a glimpse of, or a peep out of, his producer was met by his director friend's saying, 'Oh, but didn't you know – he's busy over in the States, signing up Clint Eastwood to play Hamlet. Here. Right after you've finished. At the Haymarket.' For a moment or two Alan actually believed him. That's how legendary Duncan is, as a fixer of big American stars. Once he's fixed them, he seems to have done his producer's work and moves on to other stars, wining and dining them, possibly even conversing with them.

Or perhaps he's developed a form of hypnosis that eliminates the need for more than a few sentences, one of them being an offer. When he speaks it's in a slurred voice (not slurred from drink, I've never seen or spoken to a drunken Duncan). He has a bewildering habit of confusing names, generally getting the surname right but the Christian name wrong, addressing me as Stephen, say, while referring to Stephen as Simon, a muddling process that only becomes exasperating in times of crisis. Altogether there's something very charming about him, the way he stands pulling his beard, pulling on his cigar, a bemused outsider at events that wouldn't have taken place if he hadn't initiated them.

Just before dispatching the play to Duncan, I sent a copy to Alan Bates, to whom I'd sent the first version, really for his observations as I knew he was unavailable in the foreseeable future. He'd liked it but thought it lasted dramatically – no, *theatrically* (not quite the same thing) – for only three-quarters of the journey. He responded to the new version by announcing that he was available at such and such a date, and was interested, though not yet ready to commit, at least not to a date. The only problem I ever have with Alan – and no doubt Alan has with me – is detaching our professional relationship from our personal one. I couldn't say, in tough professional terms, 'Now come on, Alan, either yes or no, we'll work out the dates in due course', if I were having a lunch full of laughter about the various disasters of life a day or so later. And Alan was always slow to get to the starting post (otherwise known as the signing of the contract) when it came to stage work. We agreed that I should suggest his name to Duncan when we met and take it from there. It would be a long, delicate process, I thought, knowing Alan. He mustn't be hurried, chivvied, let alone bullied. But the play couldn't wait for ever.

I had my meeting with Duncan in his offices, once inhabited by Ivor Novello and known as the Ivor Novello suite. I told him that the two actors I'd first thought of (during the Michael Codron days) were out of immediate contention, one about to appear on the West End stage, the other writing a book, directing a musical and acting in a film all at once, as far as I could make out, so what did he think about Alan Bates, who was interested, and was usually my first thought anyway? Duncan was ecstatic. 'Fine by me,' he said. 'Fine.' The other two actors were fine by him too, both being stars. He was completely happy to go ahead with the compressed version of Bourke and Blake, now called, as I remember, *Says He Says He*. We ruminated companionably over Alan, the delays and protracted negotiations if Alan finally decided to do it, what star should partner him, and so forth, all over a bottle of wine, there in the Ivor Novello suite, just a little down from the Aldwych Theatre, where Michael Codron had his offices. We left it that we'd wait, to an extent, on Alan, who would be a Bourke of course, and if he came through, proceed with discussions, in which Alan would be included, about a Blake.

I was hopeful, but not convinced, that a production of *Says He Says He* would one day, though not necessarily one day soon, find its way to the stage.

Shortly after Duncan and I had had this meeting in Ivor Novello's suite, which could also have been, from the look of it, Ivor Novello's bedroom, there was a phone call or a card from Jane Morgan, a director of radio dramas at the BBC. She'd done a few plays of mine with consummate professionalism – she is also a cricket fanatic, which helps our collaboration enormously. I raised the subject of Blake and Bourke. We decided I should try my hand at converting it into a radio piece, directed by herself. I only had an hour's transmission at my disposal – so further alterations and compressions were called for. The piece went out, still a two-hander, excellently performed by Jack Shepherd as Blake and Bill Nighy as Bourke. It was called *With a Nod and a Bow* and was well received, except by the *Evening Standard*, which rather oddly singled it out as the 'Pick of the Day' and then rubbished it.

For my own part, I enjoyed *With a Nod and a Bow*, thinking I'd got both the experience and the meaning for once. But I also thought, yes, that's right, it's a radio piece and I've done it on radio. It's not, even yet, for the stage. The point being, I suppose, that if you can listen to the characters without feeling a need to see their faces, watch their movements, then on radio is where your play should be. So back to the drawing board. I asked Duncan to put the production on hold and started again. I did a draft with eight characters – a synthesis, really, of the film script and the last stage version – and sent it off to Duncan, who said it was fine by him, 'God bless'. Duncan concluded every conversation with a 'God bless'. I think that, for him, the fact that a number of starry actors wanted to do it, and that Alan Bates was 'interested' – more than 'interested' – constituted sufficient grounds for purchasing the rights, which, at about this time, he did. This version of the play, which I seem to remember was called *Mr Bourke and Mr Blake*, I again put a stop to, feeling that I hadn't quite completed the process, there was a further step to be taken. The play was about there, but was both under-textured and not quite integrated. Back to the drawing board, two more drafts, three possibly, and at last I felt that I'd got it, the version I would stand by. I changed the title to *Homesick*, sent it off to Alan and Duncan, attempted to proceed with other work. Duncan phoned to say that he preferred this version to the other version even, though he'd liked that version, and the two previous versions as well, let's get on with it when we knew what Alan wanted to do, 'God bless'. I believed that the writing part of the play was finished, although there would no doubt be changes in rehearsal. A peace stole over me, a sense that I'd come through a long stuttering labour to a birth. A birth on the page, at last.

While I'd been sending out the various versions to Alan and Duncan, I'd also been sending them to Christopher Morahan, whom I wanted to be the director. He'd done one stage play of mine, *Melon*, with Alan in the lead, and quite a few television films, two of them with Stephen Fry in a leading part, one of them with Alan again. We had become friends as well as collaborators and he was, it should be said, through every phase of this exhausting process, extremely generous in his support. He was willing to direct whichever version I felt was the right one.

21

I now had a play, a producer and a director, but as yet no actors. Now and then Alan would phone up and say, 'Let's go ahead, let's just go ahead and do it'; now and then he'd phone up and say, 'You see there's this film I've got, followed by this film I've got, and I've promised to do a six-week stint at the Almeida Theatre in a mountainous part' – as it indeed was, an Austrian play in which Alan gave what was virtually a monologue, with appendages in the form of almost mute other characters. And so it went on, Alan loitering in the wings as far as my play was concerned, but centre-stage in lots of other places. I began to draw a delicate conclusion: that Alan didn't want to do the play that now rode under the banner of *Homesick*, but, being a friend, and also a kindly and sensitive man, couldn't bring himself to tell me so.

One night, I bumped into Stephen Fry at the Groucho Club, where he was dining and I was attending some function, or I was dining and he was attending some function. We had met up from time to time, but by no means regularly, since I'd directed him in my play, *The Common Pursuit*, at the Phoenix Theatre, in which John Sessions, Rik Mayall, Paul Mooney and John Gordon Sinclair had also featured. Now the fact is that before *The Common Pursuit* I'd never met, even heard of, any of these actors, although the producer, Howard Panter, had assured me that they were all famous, very talented. If I approved of them and if they approved of me, we'd attract not only an enormous audience numerically, but a new sort of theatrical audience, consisting of young people who'd probably never been to a straight play before. I was curious but cynical, cynical and yet hopeful. I met each of the suggested actors separately, at Groucho's – *The Common Pursuit* must be the only play to be cast in a private club in London's Soho. First there was John Sessions. I took to him at once – not only because of his mercurial mimicry talents but because I found something touching about him, an innocence really. He also knew my work, which further endeared him to me. The next candidate – being so much older, I thought grandly of these performers, of whose existence I was ignorant but who were, even then, much more famous than I, as 'candidates' – was Stephen Fry. He was highly articulate, intelligent and amusing, also very familiar with my work – he'd even read my novels – and had been to public school and Cambridge as I had. I signed him up without the slightest idea of whether he could act or not. What I did know was that he came from the world of the play, wanted to do the part, was a celebrity, though I'd never heard of him, and was full of confidence. I've always had a predilection for actors who, in spite of numerous other offers, want to do this or that in a play of mine. So signed up were John Sessions and Stephen Fry, with some chap called Rik Mayall, who was apparently more famous than the other two, now sitting with me at a table in Groucho's. He was freshly back from a holiday in St Lucia, was jittery, full of energy, had no idea of who I was, had obviously – no, frankly – never seen a play by me, read a word I'd written. But then I'd never seen a performance by him, to my knowledge. We were alien to each other, the more alien the more we talked. I with my malt whisky, or champagne, he with his lagers. He didn't seem to have a clue what the play was about, only wanted to play the part on offer because his chums, John Sessions and Stephen Fry, were to be in it. What could those two highly educated, semi-academics have in common with Rik, I wondered? He'd been to Manchester University, it's true, and his parents were both teachers. But he seemed positively to boast of a lack of education. John Sessions had a Ph.D., Stephen was erudite – formidably erudite, preposterously erudite, grammatically loquacious. Rik, during our evening together, sometimes gabbled, and never formed a long sequence of consecutive sentences. What I didn't realize, being ignorant of their world, was that they were bound together by a shared experience – they had all three, when young men, very young men, stood on stage before large audiences, performing comic skits and telling jokes.

I can't say I disliked Rik – I found his strange, almost innocent directness both unbalancing and attractive – but I was pretty sure that he didn't belong in any production of a play by me. After about an hour of pretty hopeless conversation, Rik suddenly said, 'Look, let's just get out of here. Let's go to somewhere normal.' He led me out of Groucho's and around several corners to a Soho pub, where he was greeted by a packed house of boozers, who identified him the moment he surged through the door. I suppose he wanted to make a point – that he was a celebrity, not just a performer, and who was that geezer (me) at the back, hanging around, with no credentials that mattered in the real world. It was a theatrical gesture, impressive in its way, as eloquent as Stephen's and John's verbal eloquence, but the anger it came out of – that I'd failed to acknowledge what he was, who he was – depressed me. I felt at that moment, as hands slapped his back, as he was proffered free drinks, that he wasn't my type.

I suppose we had further talk in that pub, but I don't recall it. I know that when we finally parted I went straight back to Groucho's, phoned the producer and said firmly that Rik Mayall was not for me, could we please look elsewhere. He was aghast. 'You're turning down Rik Mayall? You don't want Rik Mayall, probably the most popular star with the young – !' I said I just didn't think he was right as a Cambridge literary intellectual on the make. 'But he'll sell the show,' he said. 'He and Stephen Fry and John Sessions, but Rik Mayall particularly will give us full houses to the end of the run.' I spent the next day or two pondering the Rik Mayall situation. On the one hand an actor – a stand-up comedian and sit-com performer, rather – who seemed not to understand the play but wanted to mess about with his friends, and on the other a resolutely puritanical playwright/director who knew absolutely nothing about the generation of actors – if actors they were – with whom he found himself working. 'Saddled' is the word I think I used, to myself. On an impulse, without any idea of what I was going to say, I phoned Rik. 'Hello. It's me. Simon Gray,' I said. There was a brief pause. 'Yes?' he said, as if to say, 'What do you want?' Well, I wanted the right actor for a part in *The Common Pursuit*, didn't I? 'You're on,' a voice said from out of me that wasn't exactly mine, coming from an intelligence I mostly lack. 'On?' he said. 'Yes. On.' 'Well, yes, right.' He didn't sound surprised or excited – but then he hadn't been wrestling with the problem of his suitability for me and my play; he'd assumed all along that he was going to be there with his chums, bringing in thousands of his own fans – he'd pack the theatre for me, how could there be a problem?

That's how Rik and Stephen, two famous young men whose names I didn't know at the time, came into my life. Now I look back, I can see that my main casting principle was simply that I didn't have one. I'd like to think I went on hunches, but then I didn't have those either. No, really I think I was on some kind of roll. Once I'd gambled on John Sessions, I kept betting on the same number, so to speak. Although it must have seemed, and did sometimes seem to myself, that anyone who had a drink with me at Groucho's was also entitled to a bowl of olives, a bowl of crisps and, for their immediate future, a part in *The Common Pursuit*.

In Rik's case I felt sure I'd made a bad bet, until I conducted a pre-rehearsal read-through at Groucho's – not, I might say, in the teeming restaurant or bar, but in a private room off, where Rik's rendering, rasping and edgy, sometimes a snarl and sometimes almost a screech, bore no relation to the character he was supposed to be playing, I wasn't sure that he understood the meaning of many of the lines. It was then, in a state of some despair, that I *knew* I'd made a bad bet. But there was no going back. You can't fire a famous performer after one reading at Groucho's, can you? The rest of the cast were fine, which was a relief – Stephen, immensely relaxed and enjoying himself, seemed in harmony with his part. John Sessions, if strangulated and strained, evidently knew what his character was about, where he came from, what he felt from line to line. Everyone except Rik seemed to know what they were doing, which made me regret Rik all the more. Why – why – why had that unknown voice in me … ?

It's always a shock, I imagine, to find yourself the oldest person in the room when once you were the youngest. What surprised me was the discovery that this junior generation of versatile, knock-about, anarchic comics had perfect manners –

natural, easy, unfailingly warm and courteous – also serious in their work, determined to do their best by the play. Nice people, that's what they were, even if they had the impudence to be twenty or so years younger than myself. Nice people. Probably nicer than myself, by a long way. This niceness made directing them an easy enough affair on the surface – no tantrums, no jealousies over centre-stage and being upstaged, not even minor tiffs over such matters as tea, coffee, sandwiches. Sarah Berger (the only female and in an under-written part) was radiantly gentle and kind, both in character and when merely hanging about, waiting to act. John Sessions had technical difficulties – but then who wouldn't, in a part that was over-written, too autobiographical, always slightly out of focus – but enlivened the rehearsal breaks with dazzling displays of mimicry. Paul Mooney only failed on the first day of rehearsal by arriving late, having gone to the wrong place, got the wrong bus, something like that, but, though beamingly shy, I quickly learned that he was a pearl – released in his work, concentrated, he took his character to where it had to be, the very centre of the play. John Gordon Sinclair, whom I'd dismissed as too young for his part (he looked about eighteen) the instant before I offered it to him and who'd failed to increase his age by more than the few months that had subsequently passed, was so openly good-natured and so joyfully keen to get in on the action that he would jump other people's cues and erupt into scenes that had nothing to do with him. His look of bemused, cheerful apology and his squalls of laughter, as I pointed him out of the acting area, still remain a favourite memory of this time. Stephen was easy, easy in manner, garrulous, quick-witted, ever ready with jokes, asides, allusions, political opinions, but always easy – and particularly easy to get into his part, too. All I had to do was to shuffle him sideways, a few feet from his real self – although I wasn't certain that I knew what that was, so let's say the *appearance* of himself – keep him still, get him to be light with dark lines, thus making the lines darker and more painful – and he was there, dominating, tortured, self-mocking, in character. Our only bad moment came when he chose to sit himself at the piano in a far corner of the rehearsal room and thump loudly at it while I was in the middle of a scene between two other actors. 'Stephen, what the hell do you think you're doing? We're in rehearsal!' I shouted, not in anger but in astonishment. He stopped, of course, as astonished as I was by his behaviour. 'I'm sorry,' he said. 'So very sorry' – words that when he spoke them some seven years later marked a turning-point in a number of lives – 'I don't know why I – I just saw the keyboard and couldn't resist. Please forgive me. I simply forgot where I was.' This, accompanied by gestures – sweet gestures – of shame and self-mortification. I came to think of it as a comic incident, the sudden outbreak of a lonely eccentric who was unaware, for a moment, that there was anyone else in the room, or indeed the world.

The only real problem that I had when in rehearsal with *The Common Pursuit* was, of course, Rik. His voice was still raspy, although the screech had gone, but there was a dreadful assemblage of comic tricks – funny walks, shakings of his body, rollings of the eyes, meaningless mad glares – he'd imported all this stuff into the world of *The Common Pursuit*, which had no room for it. I was in despair. I knew he thought he was offering something valuable, the Rik-original-and-inventive-comic that his fans loved – and I felt there would be a kind of cruelty in refusing him the gifts he was bringing to me. What I didn't realize was that these gifts were self-protective, a disguise, and that Rik was frightened of being seen unadorned by them. He made me miserable, but I let it go for a while, too long a while really, before I decided that cruelty was the only kindness. To both of us. So one afternoon, late into the second week, I gathered all my strength and set about him. It turned out to be both exciting and easy. All I had to do was say, 'Don't', 'Don't do this here', 'Don't do that there', 'You don't need this', 'You don't need that' – a succession of sympathetic negatives which Rik accepted with a kind of welcoming relief, as if he'd hoped for this, longed for this exposure. And what was exposed, what he exposed to us in the rehearsal room, was not just that he was a true actor but that he could be a great one. Once he'd got to where he needed to be,

27

to where his deepest instincts as an actor had led him, Rik was in a state of exhilaration. And on his way to becoming a nervous wreck. He longed for an audience, the prospect of which terrified him. When we gave a run-through for the producer, the first 'outsider' to visit our work, Rik lost his lines, forgot his moves, left in the middle of a scene through which he was fluffing helplessly, for the lavatory, where he was sick. It was hopeless, he was hopeless, but I felt fine – if slightly embarrassed by the producer's embarrassment. Rik, denuded, was all raw nerve-ends, without faith in himself – possibly without faith in the play at this point – but he stuck to the path, the straight and narrow, his proper path, recollected his lines and his moves, and when we opened at Watford for two weeks of previews, glowed with confidence, his timing quite masterful, his presence electrifying, from the first moment of his entry, when without trick or ogling he made the audience alert to his presence, made them laugh by living faithfully within his character, always offering that character to the other actors to play off.

Stephen was splendid. At least I thought so, and so did the audiences; and, when we came to London, so did the critics, many of whom rated his performance as highly as they rated Rik's. On the other hand, some friends in the theatre, who admired Rik without reservation – for Harold Pinter, for instance, he was 'the bee's knees' – had reservations about Stephen. This seemed to me unfair. Stephen's slight adjustments of personality made him not 'just' Stephen Fry, but also the character he was playing, or at least a perfectly authentic account of him. He was true to the role as written, and that was good enough for audiences. For the critics. For me, if it came to that.

I've gone back to *The Common Pursuit* to explain how Stephen and Rik in *Cell Mates* came about, seven years later. Now I have to go back a year or so to my chance encounter with Stephen at the Groucho Club, where we agreed to have dinner some time in the imminent future. He'd bring along a proof copy of his latest – his second – novel, which he'd love me to read. 'OK,' I said. 'Fine. Great. I'd love to read it.' Though this heart always quivers at the prospect of having to read friends' work, as I suspect friends' hearts quiver – then possibly sink – at the prospect of having to read mine. We duly met at a restaurant local to me. Stephen was carrying a vast brief-case, which contained a proof copy of his novel, *The Hippopotamus*. Such a brief-case could house only such a treasure, which he presented to me with the lavishly humble imprecations conventional to such moments – 'Only if you've got time. Not important. Bless you, how kind of you, how sweet and kind. God bless.' It was a very agreeable dinner, Stephen on his best, evasively rich, communicative form, making me feel somewhere between a companion and a television audience. I was suddenly struck by an idea, an idea that struck like lightning, with the (though long-delayed) consequences of lightning. I told him a little about the play, wondered whether he'd be interested in reading it. So that was the current situation; he to read my shortish play, I to read his longish novel. We talked of many other things and parted eventually, full of jollity.

The next day I had my assistant, Sarah, send him a copy of *Homesick*. Some days later, after I'd finished reading *The Hippopotamus*, which I'd much enjoyed, he phoned to say he'd finished the play. Could we meet? We had dinner at the same restaurant as before, I believe, though it may have been the one opposite. I paid him compliments on *The Hippopotamus*, made a few of the almost obligatory reservations – otherwise, what value do the compliments have? I didn't say, I didn't think it was worth saying, that I disagreed with the book's premise, or rather its conclusion, which was virtually a celebration of Stephen's belief in logic, natural order and coherence, and his disbelief in what was really my own belief, the power of the irrational, the impulsive, the totally unexpected manoeuvres of an unidentifiable psyche or an unidentifiable God. All this didn't seem important at the time, certainly no more important than the later, far more explosive version of the same argument at the Ivy. He sat comfortably on his side of the table, I on mine, neither of us troubled. Not too far into the meal, he suddenly raised the issue of the play, *Homesick*. 'Look,' he said, 'is this an offer? Because if it is, I'd love to do it.' I suppose, when it came down to it, my having sent the play to him constituted an offer. We'd exchanged our latest works as fellow writers, but my work was a play, and he was an actor as well as a novelist, and that put a different twist on things. He said he wanted to play Blake. I thought at great speed, remembered him in *The Common Pursuit*, the television version of *The Common Pursuit*, his commanding and witty performance in my television film, *Old Flames*, and said, yes, right, you do Blake. I explained that Alan had been dithering for a long time over doing Bourke (remembering, as I spoke, that Alan had said frequently, 'But I realize that Blake is the better part. The part that will steal all the notices. But I'd have more fun as Bourke. If we do it.') but had now passed out of the reckoning, I assumed. Stephen's eyes positively glimmered at the thought of partnering Alan. 'Well, I hope he puts himself back in the reckoning. I'd love to work with him.' So it came about that Stephen staked his claim and I accepted it. I could see what strengths he'd bring to the part, such sweetness, such integrity, that the idea of his betraying the man who'd given him so much would be all the more appalling. The thing is, I thought, the thing is to use all of Stephen's generous and yet evasive charm in order to make Blake an *unexpected* traitor.

I reported this sudden turn of events to Duncan. He was thrilled. Stephen Bates – or possibly he said Simon Bates – and Stephen Fry – or possibly he said Alan Fry – would make a great combination. No, Alan's out of it, I said. I'm not going to pursue or harass him. He's obviously let it go by deliberate default. We'll have to look elsewhere.

I had another meeting with Stephen, said we must conclude that it was no-go with Alan, whom I'd lunched with a few days before and who had, for once when face to face, raised the subject of the play, then slipped away from underneath it, which seemed his way of putting the nail in the coffin. Let's think about Bourkes, shall we? You're first on board, have your say. Any ideas? The idea – the obvious idea – came to us simultaneously. Rik! Of course Rik! The partnership from *The Common Pursuit* revived, and possibly, given that they were contemporaries (as were Blake and Bourke), the perfect partnership for the play. 'Do you want me to go around with the script and talk to him?' Stephen asked. This seemed to me a sensible idea. Much as I admired Rik, I'd never been close to him except in the rehearsal room for *The Common Pursuit*. Stephen, on the other hand, had always had a close relationship with Rik, and wouldn't suffer the embarrassment of an author trying to persuade an actor of the merits of a play he wanted him to be in. So there we left it – Stephen would do his best to haul Rik aboard, going through the script with him, possibly even reading it aloud with him, and I could go home thinking that at last things were on the move.

Now where did this leave things with Christopher Morahan, the man who understood that he was going to direct the play? I'd cast one of the parts without consulting him – though I'd phoned him after my initial conversation with Stephen and apologized for pre-empting him. 'No, no,' he'd said. 'I like Stephen –' with whom he'd worked, it should be remembered, on two occasions on my behalf – 'I think he'll be a very good Blake.' Now I had to phone him again, to inform him that I was involved in attempting another major bit of casting, but I could stop it if he were against it, or wanted time to think about it. He didn't want time, he wasn't against it; Rik seemed to him a wonderful idea. He thought Rik was – well, the bee's knees.

Stephen phoned to say that Rik was very interested, had liked the play enormously, but couldn't commit absolutely yet, as there were films and so forth in the offing. 'But I'm sure he'll come round,' Stephen said, with such authority that he sounded like Rik's father. I reported this to Christopher, who said, 'Let's keep our fingers crossed', or words to that effect.

So that was the state of affairs in January when Victoria and I flew off to stay with some American friends – it might have been February. Duncan Weldon committed; Christopher Morahan willing to commit; Stephen Fry committed; and Rik Mayall not ready to commit, but who had made clear that he would like to be in the play, if other commitments or possible commitments didn't block his way. Things could have been worse. Far worse.

In fact I should be so lucky. Except for a small worry at the back of my mind.

The worry manifested itself in the form of a fax from my agent, Judy Daish, informing me that Alan's agent had phoned to tell her that Alan had read the play again, was keen to do it, how would August suit?

Bang! goes Fate with his fist. Bang, bang, bang! I phoned Duncan, thinking that this was another fine mess I'd got myself into. What was the state of play from his point of view?, I asked. He was unperturbed. Simon Bates and Alan Fry, Rik Bates, Stephen Mayall, any combination would be fine by him, what impressed him was that so many fine actors were queueing up to do these parts. 'But you don't see,' I said, 'don't you see where this leaves me? I know all these people. Alan's one of my closest friends. What's the word on Rik?' There'd been no word from Rik's agent, except that he wouldn't yet commit. In that case, withdraw the offer, I said, we have to proceed with our two committed actors, there was no reasonable or decent alternative. 'All right,' he said with his usual equanimity. I could see him pulling on his cigar those thousand miles and jet-lagging hours away. 'We'll go with Alan, if that's what you want. I'll go with anyone you want' – he went through the list of names, ordered God to bless me or them or the world in general, and hung up.

The trouble was, for me, as follows: I'd offered the play to Alan, who, in his silence and ambiguous references to it, had appeared to reject it; I'd offered the other main part to Stephen Fry who'd accepted it on the spot, and through Stephen I'd offered the part I'd offered to Alan to Rik. Yes, a fine mess indeed, a holiday-ruining mess. When I got back to London, I telephoned Stephen and explained the situation – that Alan had assumed the play was still on offer to him, and as he'd never officially declined it, nor had I officially withdrawn it from him, and as Rik had not yet officially accepted, I was morally obliged, etc., etc. He said that Rik had already learned from his agent that the play was no longer on offer to him, he was bewildered and hurt, he'd been going to accept, it had just been a question of dates, really, and previous commitments. As for himself, he said, he was very sorry for and about Rik, on the other hand he was thrilled about Alan. He ended on a 'God bless', I seem to recall – it was, along with 'sorry, so sorry', a signature tune in this story. I was sorry for and about Rik too. Far worse, I had a dreadful suspicion, as I'd hinted to Duncan, that, however thrilled Stephen was at the prospect of Alan, Alan wouldn't be thrilled at the prospect of Stephen. I then got in touch with Alan, a phone call I'd dreaded making, to arrange a dinner I dreaded having – the only time in our relationship I didn't want to phone, or dine with, Alan.

He brought to the restaurant a list of actors he thought would be right for Blake. It was a predictable list, a good list, but I had to tell him that the part of Blake had already gone, had been accepted by Stephen Fry. Alan blanched. He actually did go white for a second. Leaping right into the heart of the matter, he said, 'But I always wanted to do it –' meaning the play – 'I always intended to do it.' 'Why didn't you say so?' I asked. 'And save us all this confusion?' The argument between us went back and forth. He remained deeply upset, not angry but in emotional turmoil. 'So you've already signed him up,' he said. 'Morally,' I said. 'I mean, I offered him the part and he accepted it.' There was no way out with Stephen, from any decent point of view. I took up the tack I'd planned to take up: that his stage partnership with Stephen could be a very rich one. Two actors from different traditions, different generations, why, it could be for him, Alan, a refreshing experience. And for Stephen an educative one. And he'd like Stephen. Everybody did. He said yes, on the few occasions he'd met Stephen he had liked him, he could see why everybody would, but that wasn't the point. The point was that he'd reached a point in his profession where he deserved, had a right, to be consulted on casting a part as important as Stephen's – after all, Blake and Bourke were on stage together all evening. This I couldn't deny. He did deserve. He did have that right. I observed that the muddle had come about because we had a long-standing professional relationship and were also friends – if I'd been more forthright far earlier, demanding a positive 'yes' or 'no', and so back to all that over the coffees. He said, 'I don't think I can do it with Stephen. I really don't think I can.' He looked very distressed. I begged him to think about it, not to make a decision now, when he'd only just got the news. He said he would think about it, but he didn't think he could get away from his feeling that Stephen wasn't only the wrong age as his partner but, more importantly, wasn't his 'type' of actor. The next morning Alan phoned to say that he'd agonized and agonized, but was going to withdraw. He was very sorry. We hung up without 'God blesses' but affectionately and peaceably, though in fact we had to go through a couple of restrained meals together before getting back to our usual rowdy terms.

After the conversation with Alan I sat back to reflect on what I'd achieved so far as an entrepreneur. Quite a lot, really. I'd lost two stars whose acting I deeply admired. Now I only had to lose Stephen, Christopher Morahan and Duncan and I'd have run through the side, left with nobody but myself, and perhaps, with cunning and luck, I could lose me too.

I phoned Christopher – whom, of course, I'd kept informed on the Alan and Rik situation – to inform him of the minus-Alan, minus-Rik situation. He said that possibly Rik would come back. I said I didn't see why he should, he was a sensitive man who'd been treated insensitively. Anyway, we agreed that my next task was to explain about Alan to Stephen. I also had to phone Duncan to explain about Alan, but that was no task – Duncan's view being that as long as we had Stephen …

On to dinner with Stephen. I had no idea what to say and so went for the truth, sometimes the best, sometimes the worst policy. The truth being that, for reasons to do with Stephen's age (too young) and the performance tradition from which he came (too new), Alan thought they would make uncomfortable stage partners. Stephen was as upset as Alan had been a few nights before. But he was also, and refreshingly, determined. 'Let's go back to Rik,' he said. 'I'll talk to him.' Obviously his pride had been wounded. As had Rik's. As had Alan's. The entrepreneur was learning, as he went along, how to make bad worse. I didn't believe for a minute that Rik, who would feel that he'd been carelessly and callously brushed aside, would want to come forward again, even with Stephen as both bait and counsellor.

I underestimated either Stephen's influence over Rik or Rik's desire to do the part. A few days after my dinner with Stephen, Rik phoned while I was out and left a message with Sarah that I wasn't to worry, everything was going to be all right, let's meet.

Meet we did, in the bar of the Halcyon. We embraced warmly, sat down, ordered drinks and, while we waited for them to arrive, he committed himself to *Homesick*. Just like that. I struggled to look matter-of-fact, an elder-statesman figure, but I felt such a rush of relief and joy – 'You'll direct it yourself, won't you?' Well, swings and roundabouts, hills, valleys, whatever. I told him I was very keen on Christopher Morahan. Rik said he had nothing against Christopher Morahan, about whom he'd heard very good things from Stephen, but he'd assumed right from the beginning that it was going to be *The Common Pursuit* team – the three of us – again.

Many years ago, when I was a boisterous and vainglorious young playwright with successes behind me and a conviction of successes to come, I was sent to meet a star who could have satisfied the standards even of the present-day BBC drama departments. He wanted to appear in my play, but wanted the director of my choice as little as the director of my choice wanted him. I was visiting him, really, to break bad news – one of my favourite hobbies, especially if I can break it to chaps with a tendency to violence. He stared at me as if I were a freak in nature, a mouse, say, who sported a monocle and a walking-stick. He was acting, of course, but what an actor! 'Do you mean you think your director is more important than your star?' I said, yes, I did think that. In the event I got both the director of my choice, Harold Pinter, and the star of our choice, Alan Bates. But those were happier days, luckier days, when being young, boisterous and vainglorious somehow worked wonders. Now, decades later, I saw the value of the stars of my choice, and accepted a director who was not of my choice – to wit, myself – instead of the director of my choice, Christopher Morahan. Which at least gave me a chance to engage in my favourite hobby. Christopher, while disappointed, took it very well, saying he could see Rik's point; Rik knew me, didn't know him, it made sense. Stephen was also delighted, saying he, like Rik, longed to repeat *The Common Pursuit*. I was old enough to be able to say that no experience can ever be repeated, but also old enough to refrain from saying it. Duncan received this information as if it were a minor item on the back page of a newspaper, observing only that if we'd Rik and Stephen, we were in great shape. What the hell did it matter who directed, under these circumstances?, was what he was really saying, God bless. He was right. With Rik and Stephen, we'd got as close to a guaranteed success as we could get. I would simply have to undertake the thing in the world I least wanted to undertake, i.e. to direct a new play of mine. I'd sworn, to myself and to others, I'd never, ever, do *that* again. I had already passed the age when the strain, the tension, took far too much out of me, left me virtually incapacitated for months afterwards.

But still, it was finally set up. Rik as Bourke, Stephen as Blake, myself as an unwilling director. All we had to do was fix dates, cast the other parts, sign up a set designer, a lighting designer, and get on with it. Getting on with it took about a year, the procrastinations arising from Stephen, who, though committed to the play, wasn't prepared to commit himself to any date, ever. Rik, on the other hand, though equally busy, kept offering dates when he could make himself available, to no avail, as Stephen had just accepted a project for that date, another one for that date. In the end I telephoned and faxed, faxed and telephoned, Stephen's agent and Stephen himself, asking him to work out with Rik a date suitable for both of them; I would go when they were ready, but let's please, for God's sake, make it definite, however far into the future. They conferred, came up with a date – early in December – a long time away from whenever then was, but at least a date. Duncan's office began negotiations over contracts. Neither Rik nor Stephen could give more than four months of performances, a month out of town, two weeks in Guildford, two at Richmond, three months in London, at the Albery, which Duncan had booked. I gathered that there was the usual agents' competition over who should go on the right over the title, who on the left, the usual rubbish over billing, but it was eventually settled, amicably enough. Then the odd provisos popped up. Very odd provisos, as a matter of fact. Both Stephen and Rik wanted a two-week break during Christmas – thus giving us two weeks' rehearsal before Christmas, a two-week break that extended Christmas, even by British standards, into a ludicrously disruptive event, and then two weeks of rehearsals after Christmas. I'd never heard of anything like it before, and nor had anyone I mentioned it to in the theatre. 'Not serious,' they all said. 'They can't be serious', meaning seriously interested in the professionally theatrical side of things. I thought about it, the fact that they both, so I was told, wanted it written into their contracts, and decided that, well, I didn't want to get off to a combative start with my two leads and gave in on the two-weeks-at-Christmas without a fight, as a matter of policy. Other requests followed, all from Stephen's agent: a day off here, half a day off there – he was doing a pre-Christmas recording of a link-up with the stars at Christmas, had to attend this, had to attend that. To each request, disbelieving but anxious for a happy rehearsal room, and for a happy signing of contracts, I gave in.

Rik phoned up and asked whether we could have a private reading of the play before the first rehearsal, as we'd done with *The Common Pursuit*. Of course, I said, but not this time at the Groucho Club, this time at the Halcyon. Any time would suit me, when would suit him? When would suit Stephen? Would he and Stephen talk and let me know? He phoned back with a date, I arranged a private room at the Halcyon. In the meantime, I was casting the three other parts, the doubling-up parts – Carole Nimmons as the English lady doctor in Act One who becomes Zinaida, the Russian housekeeper, in the rest of the play; Paul Mooney as the socialist, *New Statesman* anti-bomb campaigner in Act One who becomes Viktor, the junior KGB officer in the rest of the play; Sam Dastor as the seedy London flat inventory-taker in Act One who becomes Stan, the senior KGB officer in the rest of the play. All of them actors whom I'd known and worked with previously. But I'd also asked them to be part of the production because I liked them, felt safe in their company and felt that Rik (who never really feels safe anywhere) and Stephen (who gave the appearance of feeling safe everywhere) would find them to be what they were – not just supportive and good, professional actors but also lively company. It was the easiest job I've ever had to do in the theatre, involving the lift of a phone, a quick drink with each of them at the Halcyon.

Of the three of them I had (on the surface anyway) the most complicated relationship with Paul Mooney, the actor who'd performed with such self-effacing brilliance in *The Common Pursuit*, and had then fallen back to his usual state, which was out of work. A year or so ago there'd been a revival of another play of mine, *Quartermaine's Terms*, and I'd persisted in pushing Paul's name at the director. He was cast on the basis of his audition, the director (Kevin Billington) agreeing that here was a very special actor. He performed well at the read-through (given the nature of read-throughs) and then – on the very first day of rehearsals – did a bunk. He phoned that evening to apologize, to explain that he couldn't come back, he'd hated the atmosphere in the rehearsal room (so had I; so had Kevin Billington) and he thought it would be better for all parties if he were to flee on the first day, rather than later. Was I very angry? Not really. He was right in thinking/feeling that if he was going to bunk, the earlier the better. Also, when it comes to it, who would want to rehearse in a poisonous atmosphere? Paul's bunk probably established him, Kevin Billingon observed, as the only sane man present (before going absent).

Anyway, to get back to Paul and his quaveringly honest telephone call – yes, he'd done a bunk on the first day of rehearsal, was fully aware that he'd let me – as his champion – down, but would I keep him in mind for anything in the future. I thought about this for a second or two, and then said that yes, I would, any time a part came up for a chap of his age he'd be my first thought. So we hung up, he back to the dole or a part-time job, I back to whatever writing I was doing at the time – probably *Cell Mates*, come to think of it. And when it came to casting the younger supporting role in *Cell Mates*, he was indeed the first person that came to mind. When we met for a drink at the

Halcyon, I put it to him pretty directly. Think about it, I said, and be sure that you want to do it. If you don't feel sure, say so, and we'll wait on another day, another year, another incarnation. He took the weekend off to make his decision, phoned me at the beginning of the next week, said he'd talked it over and over with his girlfriend and, yes, he longed to do it – and that under no circumstances would he bolt. One of the ironies that still grins malevolently out at me, as I try to come to terms with the experience of *Cell Mates*, is the memory of Stephen, who knew about Paul's flight from *Quartermaine's Terms*, now and then complimenting me on my generosity, my largeness of heart, my all-round moral 'sweetness' as a human being for honouring my word to Paul and casting him in *Cell Mates*. I couldn't really congratulate myself so fulsomely. After all, Paul left on the first day of rehearsal, making it possible to replace him without public fuss. And I cherished his talents.

My relationship with Carole was far less complicated. She's married to the talented actor Michael Byrne, who played (with laconic power) the part of Reg opposite Alan Bates in the original production of *Butley*. She was an immensely accomplished, sexy and graceful wife in *Melon* – opposite Alan Bates, somehow inevitably. To cut it short, I'd always have her in any play of mine that requires her grace and skills, and also provided that she wanted to do it.

Sam Dastor was also in *Melon*, and it was from that experience of him that I cast him in *Hidden Laughter*, myself directing. He tends to be over-precise, almost pedantic, in rehearsals, working on gestures and phrasing, every physical detail matching every sentence, but once in front of an audience he accepts directorial liberation (i.e. don't do this, don't do that) with complete equanimity – having found the character by his own accumulated mannerisms he can drop all the mannerisms and be the character. I love his expressiveness on stage – alert, questioning. He's naturally a comic, without ever struggling to seem so.

The private reading at the Halcyon went OK, I thought. Paul and Sam established an immediate rapport as the KGB officers. Paul was what I'd thought he'd be, pure and inventive in his early English scene, Sam a trifle (already, but it would vanish in time) over-elaborate vocally – too much characterization – in the inventory-taking scene. Rik and Stephen played together as if they'd known each other all their lives, but while Rik was intense, passionate, gazing towards Stephen, Stephen was light, evasive, dodging Rik's confrontations – I couldn't decide whether this was the character dodging another character, or the actor dodging another actor. But such distinctions could wait until the rehearsal room. After the reading I thanked everyone, urged wine and sandwiches around the table, and then raised the subject that I hadn't known whether I was going to, or should, raise. The two-week Christmas break. 'Two-week break. What do you mean, a two-week break?' Rik said. He was clearly appalled. 'But you asked for it,' I said. He said he hadn't. Of course he hadn't. It was the last thing he wanted, a two-week break after two weeks of rehearsals. The last thing. 'This must be Mr Fry's doing,' he said, putting his feet on the table, and staring at Mr Fry, whom he'd hitherto in my experience always referred to as Stephen or, more usually, 'Stevie', or even 'my Stevie'. His 'Stevie', suddenly particularized rather formidably as 'Mr Fry', said, well, yes, there was this problem. He had, always had had, traditionally had, heavy social engagements over the Christmas period. Most unfortunate. Didn't know what he could do about it. Might find some way – and took out of his briefcase a highly technological diary kind of thing, into which he spoke, and which spoke back at him in his own voice, reeling off his dates and obligations. Then he stuffed his self-uttering computer, in which each seemed to be the secretary to the other, back into his briefcase and, not meeting Rik's gaze as Stephen, as he'd not met Bourke's gaze as Blake, did an expansively apologetic number, very vivid. He said he was sorry, very, very sorry, he'd try to work something out, he was sure he could work something out to give us a few days more, quite a few days more, of rehearsal, two weeks was preposterous, he could see that now. Rik, with his feet on the table, kept his focus on Stephen unflinchingly, almost sardonically. I watched the two of them at it, the only time I'd ever seen a contest between them. A contest Rik had won. Also I felt pleased with myself. I'd embarrassed, was what it came to, embarrassed Stephen into recognizing his responsibilities, that he had a job to do, and other people could only do theirs if he did his. Particularly in a play that couldn't proceed without his daily participation – there was no way of rehearsing around him. Before we parted I announced formally the change of title, from *Homesick* to *Cell Mates*. I'd already mentioned this to Rik and Stephen a week or so before the reading, and they'd both come to the same conclusion – that *Homesick* was their preferred title, *Cell Mates* having a sit-com flavour to it, the kind of flavour with which they were both associated on television, but here they were in a serious play, a play called *Homesick*. I was adamant but brief about the change of title, adamant and brief because I couldn't explain my preference for *Cell Mates*, except that I preferred it.

Successful, then, as a private reading, if the future is a completely obscure place. 'So,' I said to Victoria when Sarah and I got home, 'the two-week break was all Stephen's idea, and he's going to fix that. We'll get another week or ten days. We —' meaning Rik and I – 'have embarrassed him into it.' A very obscure place, the future. But let's dip quickly into it now, to when it's become the past, to get it over with. In the second week of rehearsals I raised the matter of rehearsals over Christmas, what should our schedule be? Stephen, who'd clearly been anticipating the moment, probably prepared for it, went to his bulging briefcase, took out his high-tech diary, went to a corner of the room and spoke to himself speaking back at him, returned to the rest of us, the other actors, the stage management, me, and with great sweetness, but in this case the sweetness of regret, said it was no good, he was going to have to have the two weeks. He'd arranged Christmas festivities for a party of his friends in his house in Norfolk, there'd be fourteen of them, or forty, or 400, I can't remember, but whatever the number, it was more than I could have handled. And he was going to do the shopping, the cooking, the *placements*, the arranging of the charades, the funny readings, the serious readings, and this was going to take two weeks, otherwise counted up as fourteen days, the break in our rehearsal period he couldn't avoid. He was very, very sorry. I couldn't resist. How could I? He'd got it into his contract, I'd accepted it, he was going to do it. So much for the embarrassing of Stephen Fry. Anyway, as I've said, let's get that bit over with, as there was far worse to come, in that obscure place, the future.

Before the reading I'd signed up the set designer, Eileen Diss, with whom I'd worked often before; the lighting designer, Mick Hughes, with whom I'd never worked before, but about whom I'd heard excellent things from Harold Pinter; and Eileen's daughter, Dany Everett, as costume designer. Then there was the sound guy, John Leonard – highly recommended by the management – who was going to work out the music between the scenes and deal with all the tape-recorder technicalities. So we were finally set up, everyone in place – the cast was cast, the lighting, the set, the costumes were being thought about, the play, now called *Cell Mates*, about to go into rehearsal in a few weeks' time, out-of-town theatres and the Albery contracted. Which was when I had my breakdown. If that's what it was. I fell apart physically, psychologically, mentally – I seemed not to have the slightest idea of who I was, what I was doing, where I was going, to what end anything. I couldn't walk in straight lines, see with any clarity; I stumbled perpetually, everything was a blur – it was ghastly. Its cause lay in the immediate past and the immediate future. In the immediate past I had undertaken to write a script for a big Hollywood studio, for strictly financial reasons. 'Take the money and run,' was Judy Daish's advice – Judy Daish being my agent; 'Take the money and run,' was her advice in a nutshell. 'Train yourself to think that no film will come out of it, because it almost certainly won't.' I didn't train myself sufficiently because the subject, the poet Siegfried Sassoon during the Great War, reached far too deeply into me, overthrowing me really emotionally, so I was comprehensively overthrown when Judy's prediction proved correct: the script wasn't going to get made and, as the studio owned the rights, we had no chance of its ever being made. I was – it's preposterous to use such a phrase, but that was what it felt like – heart-broken.

The cause in the immediate future was – well, let's face it, rehearsals of *Cell Mates*. The grief behind, the nervous anxiety at what lay ahead, and of course the habitual, the years and years of too much drink, had at last made for a debilitating mixture. At a performance of the Harnoncourt version of the Beethoven symphonies, for instance, I began to blubber before the conductor had even raised his baton. I realized I couldn't conduct rehearsals in such a state – so into a clinic I'd have to go, for a week's proper rest. But first I tried to put my affairs, or rather *Cell Mates*'s affairs, in order. I had long sessions with Eileen, working through the set, I spoke at length to Mick Hughes about the lighting, and laid down the basis of what was wanted in the way of music and sound effects. Then I phoned up Christopher Morahan, the anticipated director of the play, told him that I was on the rocks, had to go into a clinic to prepare myself for rehearsals, but if things should go wrong, if I went on feeling as I felt now … I didn't have to get to the question, he cut in with the answer, he'd be 'on hold' for any emergency. I was grateful, moved and relieved by this immediate offer of support – it meant that if I went to pieces I had someone I could trust, who knew the play and who approved of all the casting, to take over. So a great weight was removed by a good friend, and a day or so later I was in the clinic.

I can't say that I remember much about the clinic, but then one is reduced to a condition, through medication, in which one notices almost nothing, so there is almost nothing to remember. On my last day, when I was out from under dosages of this and dosages of that, members of the medical profession dropped in to warn me that what I needed to avoid for some time to come was pressure. I explained that, as the playwright, pressure was unavoidable anyway, but there was no doubt that directing would double, no, triple the pressure. In that case, they said, cut right down on the spirits, which (as I knew) intensified emotional conditions, and confine yourself to restricted amounts of wine. It would have to be champagne actually, but it seemed unnecessary to correct them on this. In the event I found it surprisingly easy to keep

43

myself to one malt in the evening, though I'd been tucking into them for thirty years, and not difficult to spin out the champagne consumption. I claim no virtue in this partial abstinence. The rehearsals themselves soon became my main addiction. The day after leaving the clinic, calmly jittery, at least half-rested and only mildly retoxing, I busied myself studying the script and the model of the set which I'd taken to the clinic, and in my few moments of alertness, stared at as I imagined the actors moving about the full-scale version.

PART III

There were about twenty people in the room for the read-through, from which Duncan, who had merely come to give his greetings and 'God blesses', made a valiant effort to escape. I compelled him with sadistic courtesy to sit through both acts. After we'd finished, I felt very weak and twice as jittery, and had a desperate and panicky desire to postpone the beginning of the staging of the play, fought it, gestured the actors and stage management into the large rehearsal room, shifted some furniture, and got the process under way. There were enormous mirrors at the end of the room, so from my desk at the front I saw not only the actors, but also a reflection of myself, smoking, sipping champagne, scowling – quite disgusting. I had black cloths put over the mirrors and it was then – with the shrouding of the mirrors – that I knew that I'd be back tomorrow. At the end of the week I phoned Christopher to say I thought I was going to make it but, just to be sure, would he hang on for a few more days. In the middle of the second week I rang to release him from his vows – good timing for once, as he'd just been offered a film set in India and would have to be off there very soon. But he'd offered the safety net when I'd most needed it – nice to have staunch allies in this life. But what about the next life, will one need them there too? As a matter of fact, at this stage I would have killed in cold blood, without a second thought, anyone who tried to take the rehearsals away from me – and yet there was always the knot of anxiety in my stomach every morning that never completely unloosened itself during the course of the day and tightened again when I sat in my study at night and into the early morning, contemplating the work done, the work to be done.

45

And then came Christmas – the subject I'm not going to return to because I've already got it over and done with. So here we go again on the subject of the two-week break when Stephen was hosting and quaffing and all that stuff in his house in Norfolk – which I'd come angrily to imagine as a kind of manor, vast yet cosy. A long two weeks they were, meandering and shapeless, with no purpose to them except for Christmas Day, which was Christmas Day. The spectacle of the shops filled me, as they'd increasingly begun to do over the years, with disgust. I was plagued by a succession of corrupt images to do with our modern Christmas celebrations, all of them seeming to attach themselves to Stephen. There he was – I could see him at it with his friends – charading, guzzling, cooking, gorging. Monstrously unjust as, for all I knew, they were engaged in all kinds of pieties, singing hymns, bowed in prayer, spreading goodwill across the country – while the rest of us waited with blasphemous impatience for Stephen to return to our merely secular work where, as always, he would grace and charm us with his presence.

And return he did. With his usual grace, usual charm. And once we'd got going again, I put all anger behind me, quaffed and guzzled – no, actually merely sipped – my champagne, puffed on a cigarette, as rehearsals found their bearings, though the knot in my stomach remained unknotted, with the first night in Guildford coming up. It wasn't my fault, I told myself, that the chap Stephen Fry was Stephen Fry, the chap he was. And the chap he was was the chap one couldn't help loving, whatever. But what began to worry me was Stephen Fry *qua* actor.

To the outsider, the problem would doubtless have seemed to be Rik. He was often stammering and confused, making desperate jokes about his intellectual inadequacies, his failure to learn lines, his need for 'gags' and 'feeds'. But really he was all the time probing, probing in his intuitive way, to find 'his' Bourke. Stephen, on the other hand, was 'there' from the beginning, such a quick study that he knew his own lines too soon. In fact he knew the other actors' as well, cueing them in, reminding them of this word and that. He often also, in the most likeable and eloquently charming way, *explained* their lines to them, a procedure I could have endured with equanimity if, as the author, I'd understood him, or thought the actors were understanding him. I believe they adored his intellectual panache – they nodded and laughed in admiration, had probably never come across anything quite like it from an actor in a rehearsal room. In those moments, Stephen never gave off the sense that he was showing off – rather that he was a puppyish enthusiast for thought and speech, full of warmth and good feeling if not always of clarity. He talks to everyone on the same terms, with the same explanatory eagerness, without 'side' or pomp. He respects his audience, whoever they may be. What it seems to me he can't quite do is to talk to you as you, or him as him, or her as her. But more to the point, what he couldn't seem to do as an actor was to talk as Blake to Rik as Bourke. In other words, his acting was also fluent and easy. Too fluent, too easy. Not watching closely and, above all, not listening, especially to Rik. No, to be fair, *only* to Rik. In a number of scenes all his qualities as Stephen Fry worked in our favour – when doing his monologues into the tape-recorder, for instance, or when in a group. His address to the KGB officers on the subject of Russian champagne – his clearly fraudulent preference for it over French champagne – invariably made me laugh in rehearsal, and continued to do so in the theatre, where it brought the house down while remaining completely authentic. Also his scenes with Zinaida, his Russian housekeeper, were honest and (in the last scene) poignant. More and more poignant the more often he played it, as if he kept discovering both her and himself in an increasing depth. But with Rik he seemed forced – not forced as the character Blake, which would have been all right if not made too obvious – but forced as an actor. That's where the not watching, not listening, came in. And this crucial deficiency was emphasized by Stephen's lack of a natural stage mobility. Oddly, whenever he was on his own, he moved with a brooding, thought-immersed dignity about the room or on into his study, thus giving him great command when he did the simplest of things – sitting down at his desk, starting up his tape-machine

47

(which would never be a simple thing for me), becoming dangerous in a second of stillness. But the moment he was alone with Rik, his movements became inhibited and gauche. What was wanted in these scenes was agitation and intimacy expressed physically: movement towards each other on certain sentences; withdrawal, abrupt or slow, on other sentences; movements towards each other again – so that their bodies visually expressed, sometimes even contradicted, what was being said. But Stephen's physical self-consciousness made me tend to seat him as quickly as possible, which really meant that I had to seat Rik fairly quickly too, thus immobilizing him. A pity, but a physically fluent Rik had nowhere to go – because of the intimate nature of the scenes – except towards Stephen, and so he ended up, with rather dreary frequency, sitting beside him, physically constrained. Although not *that* constrained. Rik being Rik, his body still managed to free itself in various natural but dramatic changes of position in his chair, his head and hand movements dramatically fluent. But Stephen, even sedentary, still seemed not to be listening to Rik, and so was unable to meet impulse with impulse – he was always ahead of him, with his lines prepared, while Rik was, as always, living in the moment. No, the second. Living in the second is what Rik did. Living nowhere because he was preparing his own next moment is what Stephen did.

At one point, I found myself telling Stephen an anecdote I'd heard years ago in San Francisco. It was about an ageing Shakespearian actor who appeared in a production of a play of mine that I'd been invited over to give advice on. This ageing Shakespearian actor, who had a ghastly, throbbing, resonant, deep-bassed, sometimes growling but always, always (in my play anyway) completely hollow voice, had been, some years back, in a production of *Measure for Measure*. The director was young, innovative and secretive. So secretive that he wouldn't give the actors notes in rehearsal, and furthermore refused to let them know anything about the set design, not even where the entrances and exits would be. So the actor floundered (as all actors would, in such a situation) into despair, and finally cried out to the young director, 'Please, please help me! Give me a note, any note.' The young director took him aside and whispered an urgent sentence into his ear, whereupon the ageing Shakespearian actor rushed in distress out of the rehearsal room into the coffee room, where he was discovered by his colleagues stamping and foaming around the room, muttering in a voice no doubt less hollow than usual, 'He says "Be more *real*!" *More real*! He won't tell me where the doors are, what the set will look like, but I've got to be more *real*!'

I don't quite remember the particular context that prompted this anecdote, but I certainly know the general anxiety that provoked it from me. I was really trying to say to Stephen, 'Please, oh please, be more *real*!' About as useless a note as a director can give an actor. Nevertheless, becoming more real as Bourke was precisely what Rik was doing; whereas Stephen, in his scenes with the ever more real Bourke, seemed simply to be superimposing himself on Blake. This had the curious and (for me) demoralizing effect of making him over-present in his normal personality, and completely absent as the character in the play, at least whenever he and Rik were alone together on stage. Among the things I couldn't work out was why Stephen had always been, for me, absolutely 'real' in every scene as Humphry in *The Common Pursuit*. Could it be because Humphry was a ruthless truth-teller, which required of Stephen only that he should say his lines ruthlessly (though, of course, with his, Stephen's, natural charm); while Blake was unable to tell the truth in almost any circumstances, a liar and a traitor by nature, which required from Stephen the search for a final dot of self from whom the lies and treacheries convincingly flowed? But Stephen, anyway when with Rik, made the lies seem implausible, the treacheries inevitable – acting them, in other words, without having discovered Blake's dot of self to make them convincing dramatically. Rik, on the other hand – I'm about to repeat myself.

But then I suspect I repeated myself endlessly, and mainly to myself, during the later rehearsal period and during the early previews. One of the distressing aspects of directing your own play is that you have no one to talk to, to fret to, to moan to and laugh with over the day's rehearsal experience. If one's the writer one can talk to the director, and if the director one can talk to the writer (especially if he's still alive). But the director-author can talk only to himself, frequently with suppurating, unliberating obsessiveness. For instance, Rik and I were in the habit of stopping off at the Halcyon (which was common to both our neighbourhoods) for a quickish drink. We mainly confined the conversation to his own progress. He was always saying how worried he was about 'getting' his Dublin accent, I was always saying that the accent appropriate to *his* Bourke would evolve naturally. I would drop in tactful, I hope, notes about unnecessary bits of business – comic business, naturally. Or we'd talk about children, parenthood, our school days, early (late, in my case) sex. Once, and once only, I found myself in the middle of a sentence about Stephen's acting. I checked myself immediately of course, but not immediately enough – Rik's stricken expression made that clear. I wish, though, that we *had* been able to have the conversation. It mightn't have done much for Stephen, but it could have lifted me out of an over-suppressed gloom. On the other hand, it might have done harm to Rik, whose emotional openness – no, nakedness, really – makes him vulnerable. Quick to joy, quick to distress, all of it instantly visible in the play of his features.

It's true, as I publicly (and foolishly) stated during the later, darkest days, that sometimes I wished I could replace Stephen. I became convinced that there was a hollowness at the heart of the production. I was equally convinced that there was nothing that I (or indeed Stephen) could do about it. And two things 'happened' ...

I didn't see the first incident at Guildford, but what 'happened' was this. In Act One, Scene Two, a stage fixture on the ceiling came loose and fell on to the bed. Stephen picked the object up, revolved it quizzically in his hands, quizzically and *comically* he apparently revolved it, thus causing great mirth in the house. This, from a character who was intended by the writer to be at that moment dazed by concussion. After Stephen had finished his comic revolving of the object, whatever it was, Rik, in his character of Bourke, had to help Stephen, now completely and hopelessly out of his character as Blake, to bed. Whereupon Stephen decided to improvise.'All right,' he said. 'I'll go to bed as long as you promise nothing falls on me again.' Chaotic laughter from the audience. But as I say, I didn't see this. I was sitting in the theatre office with the Tannoy down, pondering the moves of the previous scene, and worrying about the dramatic drive of Scene Two, which at that time I couldn't bear to watch. All I had to go on was the muffled but unprecedented laughter coming through the Tannoy – and subsequently Stephen's innocently joyous re-rendering of his 'moment'.

The second incident I did see. It was at Richmond, towards the end of the first week there, I think. Blake had just announced that the KGB didn't trust Bourke. Rik, as Bourke, was in the habit of responding to this news with a gesture of panic and bewilderment, pushing away a tray on which there was a bottle of champagne and some glasses. On this occasion he pushed too hard, one of the glasses flew across the table and broke. This wasn't a big deal; Stephen had two very simple choices. One, to register the breaking of the glass as an indication of Bourke's intensity of feeling at the moment, or two, which would really have amounted to the same thing, to ignore it. But what he did – and the dialogue that led up to the pushing of the tray, the breaking of the glass went like this, by the way: 'Haven't you got anything stronger than champagne? Didn't you say something about vodka?' – what Stephen did, as he went to the kitchen hatch to order a bottle of vodka from Zinaida, was to say to Bourke, who was in a passionately discomposed state and whom he was meant to be succouring, yes, he could let him have some vodka 'as long as you don't break the glass' or 'keep breaking the glasses' or some such. This line wasn't given to Rik; it vocally winked and nodded its way straight past him, to the audience, who greeted it not simply with a roar of laughter, but with a round of applause, thus breaking whatever tension there'd been between the two characters. Rik remained resolutely Bourke, and began the long battle to get the scene back to

51

where it should be – a manifestation of his utter integrity, because if I'd been he, I'd have upped the emotional temperature considerably by attempting to throttle Stephen right there on stage. Myself, I've never been so angry with an actor in my life. During the interval, in the office, in front of Victoria and two friends of hers and Eileen Diss, the set designer, I went berserk. Quite berserk. Imprecations, oaths, obscenities – I'd almost certainly have done something cartoonish, like tried to pull my hair out, if I hadn't had a cigarette in one hand, a glass of acid-increasing champagne in the other. The company manager stepped in to announce the coming of the second act, saw the state I was in, knew exactly why, stepped out again. Victoria and her guests went into the auditorium, Eileen lingered a few minutes, calmingly, and then, when I'd climbed from rage down to despair, slipped off to her seat. Despair was the professionally appropriate response, as a matter of fact, because what Stephen's audience-captivating joke actually demonstrated was that he was so little in character as Blake in his scene with Bourke, so unconcentrated and amateurish, that at the dropping of a hat or, more precisely, the breaking of a glass, the Stephen Fry persona popped exuberantly out and got itself a wave of laughter and a round of applause as Stephen Fry. It also struck me, even in my fevered condition – I could hear, by the way, Stephen's and Rik's voices coming at me over the Tannoy – that there was another way of considering the problem with Stephen. That he looked at a Bourke and hoped for his Rik, while Bourke looked at Stephen and hoped for his Blake. The difference between an actor and an act. It was no good aiming for a hard professional-commercial attitude – that because the houses were packed, the audiences enthusiastic, we were getting away with it, let's just settle for what we've got and leave it at that. We weren't getting away with it where it mattered – mattered a great deal. At least to me. My spirits weren't raised when a good friend of mine, a film and theatre director, who'd seen the play at Guildford during a Saturday matinée (when I wasn't there, saving myself for the evening performance), phoned me on Sunday and, after the usual preliminary courtesies, asked whether there wasn't some way to get Stephen to look Rik in the eye. From where he'd sat in the stalls he'd never seen Stephen look Rik in the eye, not once. And I'd replied, 'Well, I don't know how to get him to do that. If he looks Rik straight in the eye, he'll see Bourke's eye, full of Bourkish feeling, staring straight back at him. And he wouldn't know what to do about it.' There was a pause. 'Well,' he said sympathetically, 'he's very good at being Stephen, and the audiences seem to love him as that.' And so ended a conversation we couldn't really pursue. What was the point? An actor who, on stage, simply couldn't express intimacy, seemed frightened of it, even. And off stage a warmly gregarious man, liked by virtually everyone and possibly unknown to anyone. The on-stage actor and the off-stage reality, or lack of it, connect. Snap. No Blake when needed (and certainly no Fry when needed). I suppose I could say, glibly and from a currently bitter – too bitter – perspective, that an innerly absent actor is in a constant state of defection. And that's it. The whole story. But it's not.

In the second week at Richmond, Rik, who'd had a fluish kind of virus that delivered more coughing from the stage than from the auditorium even, burst an eardrum while blowing his nose and was off for three performances. Which led to the beginning of Stephen's transformation. I don't know precisely how it happened, but my guess would be that performing with the exceptionally capable Michael Larkin, who was nevertheless an understudy and a stranger, imposed on Stephen a responsibility he had to accept – possibly accepted gratefully, as it entailed a stronger and stronger assertion of Blake's character to make up for the inevitable blanknesses in Bourke. He seemed to find a *particularity* in the scenes with Bourke at last that gave him something vastly more real (perhaps it was simply confidence) when Rik came back at the end of Richmond. Eyes met eyes, his voice had edge and thoughtfulness without premeditation, he had begun to share the scenes with Bourke as Blake and not as Stephen. Possibly he'd (accidentally) had to put himself through an intense course of education in acting. I don't mean he was actually and fully there yet, was Rik's equal in instinct and impulse – he could never be that – who, in my experience, could be? – but I felt sure that by the time we opened in London at the Albery we'd have not only the Blake we'd always had in the scenes without Bourke, but a more intimately self-revealing and boldly lying Blake in the scenes with Bourke. I felt – well, something close to elation. I also felt glad for Stephen. He could carry on from there not only in this play but in plays to come. Growing up steadily as an actor. If that's what he wanted to grow up as.

So, full of hope, on to the Albery and the first London preview. I was in the usual state of terror, stomach both churning and burning at the realization that at last we were out of out-of-town and about to face that real thing, a London audience. One of the tricky aspects of our production period was that each of our three theatres was quite different: the Guildford stage is very wide and deep, causing sight-line problems from the seats to the sides; the Richmond stage is high and shallow, causing sight-line problems from the front stalls; the Albery is almost a perfect proscenium theatre, but our four weeks out-of-town had taught us nothing technically appropriate to its sight-line problems. So, after a long day's rehearsal, we had to start for the third time as if for the first time, changing lighting, changing sound levels, rearranging the blocking, because there was no longer any excuse for blocking that had been adapted to wide, deep stages or high shallow ones. On top of which we would be playing to a London audience, who would expect a West End experience (albeit in previews at cut prices) – a houseful of amateur critics, in other words, who were there on the cheap but who would pass the word on, who would influence our future by word of mouth. We were all mostly terrified, with me (stomach churning and burning) struggling to appear the composed maestro who had been through it all before, so what's new? After the technical I gave a brief, battle-hardened speech to the troops, blasé being my mode, then retired to the nearest dressing room, which happened to be Stephen's. It was capacious, heavily mirrored, every surface piled high with letters of good wishes and premature congratulations, with here and there evidence of his high-tech expertise. A television set complete with (for me) an unworkable video system, a CD set and a pile of discs, a fax, a computer, screens and keyboards with odd lights winking, and piles of correspondence covering all the available space. Along with coffee- and tea-making apparatus. I shambled into the room, maintaining dignity, though with the usual glass of champagne and cigarette in my hand. Apart from what I brought concealingly in, there was no terror in his room at all. Indeed, he was humming and humming about the place, checking his Wormwood Scrubs costume, stroking his hair back to jailbird flatness, applying make-up. No fellow I've ever seen was more at home with himself, and this with a first preview in London coming up in under an hour's time. My job, as I understood it, was to calm him down. But there was nothing to calm down but me, which we did very well between us, me by sustaining a fraudulent equanimity, he by buzzing cheerfully from mirror to coffee-maker, humming and buzzing away, telling jokes, quoting bits of this and that from erudite publications on matters totally unrelated to the matter at hand. Rik, in his Wormwood Scrubs costume, hair slicked back, struggled into the room, every footstep a protest against his immediate future, and collapsed on Stephen's sofa. He began to howl and whine, softly, loudly, softly – then actually began to gag, awful clenching and rasping sounds from his throat, his body trembling, his complexion white through his make-up. Stephen hummed and bustled around him, now and then throwing him avuncularly ironic glances, then turning his face towards me, his eyebrows raised in compassionate amusement – 'How sweet of Rik,' he seemed to be miming. 'How sweet of him to take it all so seriously.' I smiled, amused and ironic, back at him, but in spirit I was lying gagging and groaning on the sofa, alongside Rik. I suddenly surged out of my chair, with spurious sentences of comfort to the one, of laconic confidence to the other, visited the three other actors, each of whom seemed only mildly frightened (the correct emotional condition, I think) while positively looking forward to the performance (absolutely the right mental condition) and took myself up to a little office attached to one of the boxes – Box

C, to be accurate, which I came to think of as Cell Block C, it being the place which I was incarcerated, cut off from both performers and audiences, thus making it into both cell and sanctuary – though, unlike most cells or sanctuaries, it had a bottle of champagne in a bucket of ice and a package of cigarettes waiting for me. Well, life has to go on outside the theatre, even inside the theatre. I smoked, sipped, shook slightly, and when I heard very faintly (there being no Tannoy in the Cell Block C office) the music that heralded the start of the play, I took the few steps that led to my seat at the back of the circle. There was Rik, alone on stage, seated at his Wormwood Scrubs literary editor's desk, coiled in intense concentration, completely dominating as he read and discarded manuscripts with lazy, contemptuous gestures before he began to read, with parodyingly sentimental extravagance, one of the poems – submitted by a fellow convict of great height and strength, with a violent temper, we discover subsequently – and enter Stephen, neither focused nor unfocused, bland, genial, partially observant, but somehow – as always – very present. And the play proper began, although the interplay didn't, quite. This short scene, about eight or nine minutes long, in which the two characters meet for the first time, explore each other from what seems to be instinctive affection, but with very different needs, was certainly better than it had been at Guildford and early Richmond, but not as good as late Richmond, when Rik had come back from his burst eardrum, after Stephen had worked with Rik's understudy. But it was helped by the blocking, which I'd changed for the almost perfect Albery – more fluent and relaxed, but lacking tension – so too fluent, too relaxed, in spite of Rik's palpable intensity. Stephen's main concern, from the author/director point of view, seemed to be to nanny Rik through the scene, six foot three of Valium really, while what Rik really needed was an intensity to match his own. That he was all nerves was appropriate to the scene. What he needed was someone to make him nervous. Well, we'll go back to somewhere further on tomorrow in rehearsal, I thought, as my own nerves settled, letting my eyes flick around the house. Every seat was taken, there was standing room only, and a lot of people were standing in the standing room. When I got momentarily bored with the play, I galvanized myself back into it by estimating my double percentage, one as author, the other as director, so reminding myself that I had a job of work to do here, that my little torch, my pen and my large yellow pad were all for doing that work with, in the form of note-taking. Dutifully, therefore, I switched on the torch, took notes, and struggled to keep my mind off the financial gains, not enormous (as Rik and Stephen had only contracted for three months in the West End and I saw no chance of replacing them) but enough to see me through a desperate patch, after five years, on and off, of writing the play, three months and a bit of rehearsing it, supervising its out-of-town performances, during which I gave notes, notes, endless notes – and here I was, still making notes during the penultimate (i.e. first!) preview. One more preview, one more notes session with the actors and stage management – but until then no leisurely and self-indulgent distractions to do with money and puritanical bank managers; keep to the task.

The rest of the performance went well, with the usual (uselessly written down) provisos about Stephen in his scenes with Rik. I shared the interval in Cell Block C with my agent (Judy Daish) and Duncan's associate, Peter Wilkins, whom I sometimes thought of as a kind of henchman – it seemed invariably to fall to him to do the management's dirty work and clear up afterwards, which accounts, perhaps, for his sometimes blustery manner, which in turn accounts for my inability to visualize him physically. For instance, does he have a beard or have I merely attributed a beard to him because Duncan has one? Anyway, there was Peter Wilkins, whether bearded or beardless, but not, as I recall, Duncan himself, who, fully bearded, was doubtless conducting business elsewhere, probably in the form and shapeliness of Raquel Welch, who was appearing in *The Millionairess* at Guildford. But then again out of Cell Block C and back into the auditorium. More notes. Final curtain. Good reception. I hurried back-stage through various secret corridors and channels, having told the stage manager (still, then, David Bownes) that I'd like the company to linger on for half an hour or so while I dished out my pages of notes. Which I did. My main intention was not to change anything very much – not much needed changing, and what needed changing couldn't be changed except from Stephen's stepping back, metaphorically, to where he'd been at the end of Richmond – but to be pragmatically professional. This is what we do on the first preview in London, is what I said. And this may well be what we do once or twice a week after we open. It's our job. All there is to it. Don't worry. We're pros, yes?

Of course, we all knew that two previews before the official – the press – opening in a new theatre were nothing like enough to play the play in all over again. The management had decided, nevertheless, that two previews were all we could have, the alternative being some fifteen or seventeen previews (all, it has to be remembered, at reduced prices) because between our second preview and our fifteenth preview the press were committed to nothing but other people's first nights. Bad management here, on somebody's part. I tend, from habit, to blame the press. Equally, from habit, to blame the management.

I don't remember much about the second and final preview. I assume that when I wasn't watching the play and making notes, I was in solitary confinement in Cell Block C. But this might have been the evening in which Stephen, having fallen down the wall of Wormwood Scrubs, gashed his head and torn his prison uniform, turned up in the London bedsitter with an immaculate bandage, looking like a slightly drugged caliph in a truncated turban, and in an uniform that looked as if it had been purchased half an hour previously, from a fashionable tailor, or Harrods, even. I mentioned the uniform, with a reasonably controlled temper, to the stage management. What had happened, it seemed, was that Stephen had passed his prison garments on so that he could have a second pair completely broken down into which he would change during the scene change. The girl to whom they'd been passed hadn't been given clear instructions, thus assuming that her responsibility was to send them to the cleaners for an exactly reverse process – i.e. laundered, ironed, stitched, so forth. With the show on the point of starting, it was discovered that Stephen, far from having two prison uniforms, one fairly clean for the first scene, one tattered from his tumble down the wall in the next scene, had no prison uniform whatsoever. Crazed phone calls were made to the dry cleaners in question, emissaries were sent, the one uniform, immaculately reconditioned (it was pretty immaculate – too immaculate in my view – to begin with), was somehow delivered to the theatre at the last possible moment, and there was Stephen, sprucely garmented in the first scene, a model, one might say, of a well-dressed British convict – a just about plausible proposition – and then in the next scene in exactly the same uniform, having fallen down the Wormwood Scrubs wall, bashed his head, scraped his knee, lost buttons and lapels, implausibly immaculate. That's my memory of the second preview. Although it might have been on the first preview. But one night or the other it certainly happened. I suppose I gave the usual different notes. I've long realized that after a certain point it doesn't matter what detailed notes you give, only the large ones ('Be more real') matter, because the small ones rectify themselves as a matter of course, while introducing others that on the following evening rectify themselves as a matter of course. On the whole, actors note their own notes, correct themselves as they go along, make fresh mistakes which they then correct. Nevertheless, they *need* to be given notes, to feel that they're being watched, chided, and therefore cared for. And some notes are actually useful as hints towards the larger, unspoken notes ('Be more real'). The only real issue, in one of the two previews, that required emergency measures was Stephen's prison uniform – his *two* prison uniforms.

And so on to the next night, to the offical first night, the press night. I came in early, holding a carrier bag, wearing my Loden overcoat, which I kept buttoned up as I presented myself to the company in Stephen's dressing room. I gave and received the usual warm greetings, then turned away casually, unbuttoned my coat and stood revealed in my smartest suit and most sparkling black shoes, but wearing, instead of a gleaming white shirt, a sweatshirt on which was inscribed in bold letters

'Wormwood Scrubs', where it had actually been manufactured. This was a present from Judy, via her assistant, who was a prison visitor. Judy had appeared on the doorstep that morning with a cornucopia of Wormwood Scrubs gifts – the genuine articles: a toothbrush, a towel, a razor, a mug and a plate, and a picture painted by a convict, signed 'Mr Griff, Wormwood Scrubs '95', of Rik and Stephen as Blake and Bourke, imagined from newspaper interviews, photographs, etc. The sweatshirt, my standing proudly in it, thrusting my 'Wormwood Scrubs' chest out at them, released an explosion of hilarity – perhaps because they thought that I'd finally admitted that I knew where I belonged. Anyway, it made it easier to get down to business. 'Look,' I said, having discovered that Rik and Stephen between them had about thirty friends coming in, the rest of the cast another thirty or so, 'Look, there are a lot of friends out there –' I had one or two of my own – 'and quite a few enemies – and a lot of critics and ordinary punters who just hope they're going to have a good evening in the theatre, for which they've paid good (or ill-earned?) money. But you don't play for any of them, not my friends or yours, not to the enemies, not to the critics, not even to the well-wishing but initially neutral audience; you play to each other. And if you feel a need to play to an eye and an ear in the auditorium, you play directly to me. Which means you ignore me completely and play to each other. Be arrogantly and concentratedly in the play. There are no friends, family, critics, nobody, not even me – just yourselves in your own world, leading your own lives on stage.'

This speech went down especially well with Stephen and Rik. Rik has always had a healthily aggressive attitude to his hostile critics, referring to them snarlingly as 'the fuckers', while Stephen had famously, only recently pronounced that he'd completely stopped reading newspapers, of any sort – for which he was inevitably attacked in the newspapers, one journalist being so incensed that Stephen wouldn't be reading his newspaper diatribe against Stephen's refusal to read newspapers that the article had something rabid – and certainly surreal – to it. I told Stephen – we were still in rehearsals at the Old Vic at the time –

about the piece, and how much I'd enjoyed the paradox of the journalist's predicament, his 'infuriated frustration', I think were the words I used. He was delighted, crowing, manic in his response: 'I knew they'd do that! I *knew* they'd do that!' he kept repeating, almost dancing around the rehearsal room. It struck me suddenly that I'd been pretty stupid – after all, what's the point of giving up reading newspapers if some clown (like me) doggedly reports on what's in them. Anyway, back to Stephen's dressing room, and my rousing, if slightly over-familiar (to me, anyway) peroration. When I'd finished there was a moment of sudden silence, sudden warmth – a room full of the intimacy of a long-shared experience. I toasted them all huskily, with my, on this occasion, completely justified glass of champagne. I like to think they'd have toasted me back if they'd been allowed to drink – or allowed to be *seen* drinking by their champagne-swigging director. The meeting – our last important professional meeting – broke up in a dishevelled exchange of first-night presents. Mine was an easy task: I gave everyone connected with the production a freshly published copy of the play with (I hope) an appropriate dedication. Stephen, somehow characteristically, had bought everyone a Fortnum and Mason's hamper full of vodka, caviare, etc., while Rik, equally characteristically, dished out dildos, etc., that he'd obtained from his local sex-shop. *Our* local sex-shop. I never knew there *was* a local sex-shop and I still don't know where it is – not, I'd like to make it clear, that I've searched for it. To me he gave a formidable plastic cap gun, to go after 'those fuckers' with. I can't imagine that he got *that* from the sex-shop, unless there are forms of perversion with which I'm completely unfamiliar. The present that struck the deepest chord was a cricket bat – no, *the* cricket bat, one I'd jokingly implored David Bownes (company manager) to bring in to rehearsals. There it had been the next day. Either I had complete faith in David Bownes's response to even jokingly expressed needs or it was a coincidence that there was a tennis ball in my pocket – actually I now remember that I'd been carrying it about for a few days, bouncing it up and down in rehearsals, during pauses for thought, so the fact of the ball probably came before and provoked the thought of the bat. So there we were, with a bat and a ball. What more could a playwright, a director, five actors and four stage management want? We did a bit of batting and bowling, but really I regarded them as having some moral as well as playful purpose. But what moral? To keep a straight bat? To keep our eye on the ball? To play up, play up, and play the play? Needless to say, when we went on to Guildford for our performances there, I completely forgot about the bat, except once, in the theatre office, when I had a sudden memory-glimpse of it, propped against the wall of a rehearsal room now occupied by others, without purpose either playful or moral. But now, at the first-night exchange of presents, the bat was back, presented to me with the names of the company written all over the blade, starting at the top, in a large flourish, with the name of Duncan C. Weldon, a name that always seemed to be from the past in that one could never quite remember when one had last seen him. And all the other names – the bat is within sight as I write this, along with other *memento mori* from *Cell Mates* – there's David Bownes's, from whose inspiration the gift came, Paul Mooney's, Carole's, Rik's and, eye-catchingly, Stephen's, with two crosses which I take to be kiss signs underneath it. I was very moved by this gift, although it arouses vastly more complicated feelings when I look at it these days. As I've just done. Here, in my study on 1 April (of course!).

So, back again to Stephen's dressing room that first night, where everything was finished – pep speeches, present-exchanging, seriously affirmative cuddles. All that was left to perform was the performance, and that no longer had anything to do with me. After all, I couldn't control the technical matters, the sound, the lighting, the cue lights; nor could I shout notes out to the actors in mid-performance; it was too late to rewrite any parts of the text or alter the curtain call. I was on my way to being a free man again. A writer again – so not a free man, an enchained one. But at least self-chained.

I stayed in Stephen's dressing room to change from the Wormwoods Scrubs sweatshirt into the proper one, the gleaming white cotton number I'd brought in the carrier bag, and set off for the Ivy where I'd arranged to meet Victoria. On my way there, I reflected that apart from physical problems nervously occasioned, bewildering jumps from constipation to the squitters, my bouts of depression, the chaotic and ill-fated journeys ('jinxed' is I believe the word I used to describe them earlier) – apart from this, apart from that, *Cell Mates* was unquestionably the most good-natured, the most steadily, progressively harmonious production with which I'd ever been associated. It was also going to be a triumph – how could it not be with Rik Mayall in the lead, giving an astounding performance, with the famous and beloved Stephen Fry, who seemed to me to be on the brink of giving a really fine performance (in the second preview he'd picked up where he'd left off at Richmond)? And, of course, there was a splendid supporting cast. We were bound to get some good reviews, and we didn't even need those, except for our vanities. This wasn't complacency; we'd all worked extremely hard, though happily, to put the best that we could into the West End. No, not complacency. Far worse than that, as it turned out. It was *hubris*.

I plodded to the Ivy, unaware of my *hubris*, unaware that the gods had a sardonic eye trained on my progress. They were still studying me, no doubt, as I had a drink with Victoria, and then escorted her (or she escorted me, or perhaps we both simply escorted each other) back to the Albery. When we got there, five or so minutes before curtain-up, the foyer was throbbing with first- nighters, some of whom, I hoped, had paid for the privilege. I spotted David Bownes standing by the box office – or, more likely, he spotted me, caught my eye, drew us towards him. He gave me our tickets, which I passed on to Victoria, as I had a habit of misplacing them in a pocket I didn't know existed, or of just letting them drop from unwilling fingers. We sat on a bench there, either by or actually in the box office, waiting for the ushers and usherettes to shift the crowd to their seats.

I'd given very precise instructions. The curtain was to go up as close to the announced moment as possible. First nights tend to be oddly inconsequential social events, with the play squeezed in between prolonged chat and laughter at the various bars. The curtain-up is delayed and delayed, people drift gossipingly down to their seats, which they have trouble, though they seem not to mind that, locating, settle interminably down as they rustle through their programmes to discover which scene they're starting at, possibly even which theatre they're at. Well, I'd decided, after nearly thirty years in the theatre, I was going to have no more of it. At least this once. The audience was ushered and bullied into the auditorium almost to the advertised minute.

Victoria and I were about to follow them when a swarm of photographers came buzzing into the foyer and stood, with their backs to us, positively blocking us into our box-office bench as they clicked and snapped and flashed away at the late, and I trusted last, arrival, who turned out to be, as I discovered when I finally managed to glimpse her, a famous television star. When she was allowed to pass, or perhaps when she allowed the photographers to allow her to pass, thus allowing us to get up from our bench and follow her into the auditorium, the curtain-up had been delayed after all. Furthermore, I suspect the impression given to the audience was of a strutting playwright making a late entrance while testing their patience. The music began, the lights went down, the curtain went up, the gauze went up and there was Rik, alone on stage, thumbing his contemptuous way through a clutch of poems.

I struggled to contain, unsuccessfully, a coughing and sneezing fit. Along with some gaping and raucous yawns. My nerves always manifest themselves in this way. I have to struggle not to be the most obstreperous member of the audience at my own plays, in the meantime scowling murderously at anyone who as much as adjusts a buttock or pats a partner's knee. But I did settle down at last, subdued by Victoria's tight clasp around the wrist nearest to her, and concentrated on the play, the performances.

There wasn't that much wrong with either that I could see or hear. Rik was too gesticulatory and fidgety, too manically anxious to get on with his life as Bourke, but the passion was there

64

all right, the neediness, the loving opportunism – just a lot of unnecessary hip-jouncing and digital work – first-night stuff, in other words, which brought out all his physical exaggerations, though he still managed to keep the inner Bourke intact and visible. Stephen, well, slipped back a bit into being Stephen. What one had expected from *his* first night, and which one knew he'd overcome in a night or two. The rest of the cast were solidly rooted, consummately professional. There were the usual longueurs during the set changes, though fractionally less protracted than in previous performances. The truth about the longest longueur was that it was caused not by the stage-hands or a designer's over-complicated set, but by Rik, who had a mystical relationship with his costumes – or rather his two costumes, as after Act One, Scene Two he didn't have a proper change. But after Act One, Scene One he had a serious change, from prison garb to street togs. He would not, he simply would *not* go on stage in Act One, Scene Two until he was convinced that he'd completed the transformation perfectly – from convict garb to London togs, from hair this way to hair that way. Furthermore, he wouldn't accept any form of cheating in his two costumes, so he couldn't get the first one off quickly, and wouldn't put the second one on quickly. This created an infuriating hiatus between the first two scenes, all the more infuriating in that the first scene, as I've already mentioned, ran for only eight minutes, and then all the more infuriating in that the set and Stephen were ready for Act One, Scene Two to begin. Stephen, after all, also had a tricky change, out of his fresh prison uniform into his tattered one. But there it was. Rik stuck to his meticulous method with his uncheated costumes, convinced that bad luck would befall him, his performance would suffer, if he didn't. So whatever he felt about other people's superstitions (i.e. *Macbeth*), he honoured his own to a fanatical degree. There was nothing I could do about it except be grateful that he had only the one change. Unlike Stephen, who managed them all with speed and efficiency, and a realistic willingness to cheat, when necessary. But then I remember recalling yet again, as I sat through this first set change, cursing it as usual, how different Rik and

Stephen were, not only in their personalities but in their professional attitudes. When we moved into the Albery for the technical rehearsal, Rik, every time there was the slightest break for a lighting or sound adjustment, would rove about the stage, making himself more and more familiar with it, while simultaneously checking every part of the auditorium, the stalls, the tiers of circles. Stephen, during the same breaks, would lie on the onstage bed, his arm over his eyes. An example of the hedgehog (who knows one big thing) and the fox (who knows lots of little things), except that the fox was recumbent in a position associated with hedgehogs, and the hedgehog was prowling the terrain, eyes alert to all possibilities of both prey and danger, in a manner usually associated with foxes. For me, Rik on stage during that process is one of the most vivid images of the experience of *Cell Mates* – a star working on the practical techniques required of stardom.

At the interval we hustled ourselves up to Cell Block C, where to my surprise, indignation even, this little room in which I'd spent many solitary hours was abuzz with people. The theatre manager was giving a private party. Among the official guests were the producer, Duncan Weldon, his associate, Peter Wilkins, and the theatre manager himself – affable, welcoming – most generously urging me into this little party to which, as author and director, I'd naturally not been invited. The feeling was one of restrained liveliness. We stood around drinking champagne, some of us (i.e. myself, and possibly Duncan on a cigar) smoking. Nobody seemed to have much to say to anyone, apart from a gregarious corner in which the theatre manager clustered around his guests, whoever they were, who were talking loudly amongst themselves about matters that seemed completely unrelated to the occasion itself. I supposed they were celebrating the interval for what it was – a short passage of time between getting away from somewhere they didn't want to be before returning to the same place. Duncan suddenly confided that he thought it was going very well, the box office was doing momentous business, standing room only again, and probably tomorrow (Friday night) and the two Saturdays were pretty well sold out. He looked his usual self, shyly absent-minded, and thus somehow reassuring. Peter Wilkins offered boisterously reinforcing compliments, the Jewish Weldon and the gentile Wilkins in complete synchronization when addressing the quarter-Welsh, quarter-English, half-Scots but temperamentally totally Welsh author/director, who had nothing to offer in return except mumbles, grins and grimaces, while attempting to maintain a convivial and confident manner. But really I couldn't make out what I or the company had in common with a chap and his associate who were scarcely ever encountered on the premises of the theatres we appeared in – who were they, this pair? Of course I knew exactly who they were. They were the chaps who made it possible for chaps like me to get plays on. This thought made me look upon Duncan and his cigar, Peter Wilkins, whether bearded or not, with sudden affection – admiration, even. They might be the 'business' in show business, but without their business there wouldn't be a show. So – so – let this pass, I thought, let this evening pass as best it could – and then on to the next. If there is a next.

I'd made sure it was a very short interval – i.e. kept to the minute – as it can be even more damaging to have a delayed start to the second act than to the first. Before the play starts the audience doesn't know what the play is about, which is better than their forgetting what it's about half-way through. I studied the theatre manager's slightly gangsterish (but probably only stooped-with-responsibility) back, puffed on my cigarette, held Victoria's hand from time to time, slurped down some champagne, until David Bownes came in on the dot of the second bell to announce curtain-up, and I, with what I hope were polite gesticulations, ushered the contents of the room back to their seats – it's generally the private party, having just opened a second bottle, or a third, that holds things up. For once the whole audience was obedient to the bells – nice for the ushers and usherettes, who therefore didn't have to behave like their colleagues at Covent Garden Opera House, who are forced to drop their perfectly civilized manners for a few moments and adopt the air of bouncers, seeming positively to threaten people back to their seats. On the first night of *Cell Mates*, at the Albery, the second-act curtain rose when it was meant to rise, unimpeded by photographers and the television star, who either was minding her manners by being punctually seated or had taken the opportunity of the interval to depart from the theatre.

I don't recall much of the second act, being mainly concerned with ticking the lines away, the scenes away, just wanting the whole thing to be over with, really. And in due course, to the right lighting cue, the proper curtain-call, it was over. There was the traditional scuttling of the critics up the aisles, which suddenly seemed to resemble gutters, while from all over the auditorium came the right amount (i.e. generous) applause. I know it's the view of some of the critics that first-night audiences are 'fixed', the houses filled by the cast's extended families, along with bank managers and other hopeful creditors, but I don't believe this to be true, not with productions of my plays anyway – which have been very badly received, quite badly received, quite well received, very well received, from the beginning to the end of their respective journeys. First-night houses carry 'paper' – that is, free seats for reasons of courtesy or finance (and critics are, in a sense, a double sense, also 'paper') – but disappointment is disappointment, expressing itself as such, and enthusiasm is enthusiasm, expressing itself as such. This doesn't mean that both the enthusiasts and the disappointed might not have second thoughts. After a short stint as a theatre critic, I vowed never to do it again, as I kept having second, fifth, ninth thoughts about a play I'd reviewed unfavourably. If a play went on living in the memory, it had already achieved something memorable. I can't say I had any second thoughts, or any thoughts at all, about *Cell Mates* when the first night was over. I enjoyed the audience's display of appreciation, as I'd enjoyed it over the last month, then grabbed Victoria's arm and hustled her out, around to backstage. The dressing rooms were already filling up, the hugs and cuddles and kisses under way, the bottles popping open.

After we'd done the rounds we headed to the party at Groucho's. Everyone connected with the production had been invited, along with friends, relatives, agents and so forth. When we went into the main room there was a great deal of applause. Clapping at first-night parties is a New York habit, imported by the likes, I suspect, of Andrew Lloyd Webber in their increasingly successful attempt to turn the West End into Broadway, not only on the stage but off it, in publicity-scrounging rituals and celebrations. Such applause in a private place doesn't feel right in London, and also hangs about in ironic memory, as it is currently hanging about in mine, long after the memory should have thinned down to fond recollections of the tributes one could take as genuine.I made some quite meaningless stoops of the upper half of my body, in imitation of bows and thanks, and demanded, rather too loudly, a drink, any drink, as long as it was a malt whisky of Glenfiddich brand, with two lumps of ice dropped in. Victoria and I moved about and moved about, then separated to different social chores. Stephen appeared, after a long session in his dressing room with his family and chums, Rik appeared later, after a longer session – both to terrific applause, in which I joined, thinking it would be churlish for the author/director to stand with his hands occupied with his vices, the only person in the room refusing to acknowledge the two stars. Among the people who turned up was Simon Ward, hurrying in a little late since he was in Lonsdale's *On Approval*, just down the road from the Albery, and with whom my life had been entwined professionally since my first stage play, *Wise Child*. Little did either of us know, as I greeted him with the warmest of hugs, that our lives were about to be professionally entangled again, in only a few days' time. And then came Harold and Antonia Pinter, regal, jovial (but where had they been between the end of the show and the party? Unless, of course, they'd only pretended to go to the show and done something more sensible and entertaining instead). Harold grasped my arm with strange, almost merciless ferocity and said, 'Well done' in a dark, gravelly voice. His voice is naturally dark and gravelly, but here it was darker, gravellier, which gave his utterance a hint of ambiguity. But it was the right gesture, they were the right words …

Stephen's parents were, in their words, 'bursting with pride'. They said they'd never cared as much for anything Stephen had done before, but now, here he was, showing the world he was a real actor. It was almost as if they were celebrating their son's coming of age. I looked towards Stephen, who was now sharing a table with Rik. They were obviously into one of their double acts, spiralling together down – or is it up? – into the nursery. It occurred to me that the only way this couple – and they did make a sort of couple (off stage anyway) – on the one hand this volatile, emotional and nakedly expressive man, and on the other, a man slightly cloaked, in a constant public personality – no, no, it's a *semi*-public personality, that sense he gives of sharing with great generosity half of himself, without giving you the slightest idea of what the other half is – anyway, the only means Rik and Stephen, those very different beings, could find to express their mutual affection was through the delirium of their nursery turns. So there they were again, making what looked like very necessary contact – both of them high on the experience of the evening, exalted by the public and the private applause, clinging to each other, loving each other, feeding each other – hysterically united although in every aspects of their real natures probably quite separate.

I caught Victoria's eye and indicated departure was now socially OK – which meant another half an hour of goodbyes. What is that quote from Samuel Butler? – 'It's not the farewells I mind, it's the leave-taking', something like that. I eventually managed to call a taxi, and home we went, jiggity-jig.

I describe all this because it was such a *normal* first-night party. I mean all first-night parties are abnormal events by definition, but this was a normal abnormality. Nothing in the wind, no omens or portents. I can't say I felt calm – calmness being an emotional and physical condition that's always eluded me. Nervous tension in my work, dread about the fates and fortunes of those I care for, guilt for sins committed, sins I'm both fearful and hopeful of committing being my daily and nightly inner style. But, the fact is, I knew, 'in my blood and my bones', as Rik's character says in the play, that I'd produced something that I'd longed to produce since I'd first started writing. A critic-proof production. It didn't – it really didn't – matter in the slightest what the 'fuckers' said. *Cell Mates* had played to packed houses in Guildford, Richmond, the two previews in London, and for its three-month season it would continue to do so. So, out of the ghastly financial doldrums at last. I could even almost afford the ten-day holiday I'd booked in Barbados, where Victoria and I would sit in the sun, go swimming, even hop about on the dance floor. So it had clearly been worth it, the long period of writing (but that's always worth it, the activity in itself, I mean) followed by the year of frustration setting up the production, the time I spent in the clinic getting physically strong enough to take on the direction, then the daily strain and tension of rehearsals, the miseries of travel by taxi and train, the early hours of brooding over lines and scenes that didn't work, the churning – almost gastric – frustration over this or that aspect of the production – *all* worth it. Especially as I was pleased with what was on the stage. As I said to Victoria over and over in the taxi, all worth it.

On Friday the reviews started to appear. Over the years I've developed a method of avoiding the unnecessary pain caused by reading bad reviews, by not reading them. Sarah and Judy vet them for me and point me to the ones that will either interest me or even give me pleasure. I was warned off a couple of them, the *Standard* being one – 'Really quite mild compared to what he writes about me,' said Harold when he phoned to arrange a cele-bration lunch. By Saturday, we had five perfectly decent – more than decent in several cases, and all of them decently long – reviews in five leading national newspapers. On the coming Sunday there would be only the *Observer*, which I wouldn't need Sarah or Judy even to vet (their reviewer johnnie has never liked anything I've written, so why should he start now?) and the *Independent on Sunday*, along with the *Sunday Telegraph*, both of which turned out to be warmly disposed, though the *Sunday*

Telegraph had a reservation about Stephen. The other Sundays would carry nothing until the following Sunday, by which time I would be out of the country, further reviews probably unobtainable and anyway a matter of complete inconsequence. We already had enough quotes – more than I'd received on previous occasions for plays that had had very decent runs – to make for a resplendent front of house and to decorate the ads, and my only complaint was that the rest of an exceptionally fine company scarcely got a mention. On the other hand, they had the consolation of knowing that they were in a hit. So it was a jaunty company I met jauntily up with on Friday evening. I dished out a few notes, then up to Cell Block C, then a brisk trot down to my usual seat from which I surveyed the standing-room-only full house.

After the performance I collected my first-night presents – my Wormwood Scrubs sweatshirt, Stephen's hamper, Rik's gun, the cricket bat, the cards and letters – and over-burdened, agitated with satisfaction, I set off for the Ivy. As I wended my way through the restaurant towards Victoria, I suddenly knew that something was amiss, or that there was something I'd missed. It was like a squeeze in the stomach, a stab to the loins, but not physical and not quite premonitory. I stopped for a second, I felt myself blinking, then went over to the table. 'What's the matter?' Victoria asked. 'You looked haunted.' I think I said something vague – 'Nothing, oh, nothing, just someone walking over my grave sort of thing.' She wondered if I were worried about anything. 'Nothing,' I said, 'Haven't a worry in the world' – clearly untrue as I had a number of quite specific matters to worry about, none of them connected with the play, and even when you don't have specific worries, there are the ones you didn't know you had to worry about – standing beside you, waiting to clasp a hand on your elbow, coming up behind you smiling at your shoulder blades with knife in hand, coming around a corner and straight towards you in the form of an out-of-control lorry or a learner driver with an inebriated instructor or – when it comes to it – sitting next to you in the Ivy, currently radiant and healthy-looking. There's worry connected to whomever

72

you're connected to in life, and much of it has nothing to do with putting on plays. But what the hell, what can you do about it except worry of course, have dinner, take a taxi, and home again, jiggity-jig.

I have no recollection at all of what we did on Saturday. Without doubt I played a lot of CDs (I always have music going in my study; sometimes I actually listen to it), made and received phone calls, might have gone to a film or had dinner somewhere – certainly went out because when I got in there was a message on the answering machine from David Bownes, saying that both the matinée and evening performances had gone extremely well. Furthermore, Stephen had been magnificent, even in the scenes with Rik, by far the best performance he'd yet given. At the end of the second show Stephen and Rik had gone to Groucho's, presumably, I assumed, to celebrate this particular passage in their careers, their lives. So all that was OK, was fine, no stomach-clutchings, no loin-stabbings, just a slightly avuncular pleasure at the thought of the two lads turning it on for each other until well into the following morning.

On Sunday, after a struggle to get out of bed, I remembered my directorial duties and phoned Rik, who wasn't in. I then phoned Stephen, on whose answering machine was an opaque but chilling message: 'I'm sorry,' the message said, 'I'm so very sorry.' The dead gloom of his voice was so distressing that I thought it must simply be an over-accomplished joke. And even if it weren't, I couldn't believe, given Stephen's multi-faceted life, that it had anything to do with *Cell Mates*. On the other hand, I didn't quite believe it was a joke, and also didn't quite believe that it had nothing to do with *Cell Mates*, otherwise why would I have left jocular assurances about his performance, its continuing growth, assurances that weren't bogus in content, but were – I felt – bogus in tone, as if attempting to conceal from the two of us my anxiety about him.

I tried to put his message out of my mind, but couldn't. It hung about worryingly, the worry, for some hours. In the late afternoon I asked Victoria to phone him. 'Tell me,' I said, 'what you make of his message.' She listened to his answering machine, looked at me, puzzled. 'Well, I don't see what's wrong with it.' I took the phone from her, dialled him again, and there was his voice, giving the time of his message – 5.40 p.m. – and going on to say that he would be out for the rest of the day, not back until very late in the evening. So that was all right then. Though I didn't quite believe that either. Especially as it was exactly 5.40 when I phoned, by my watch, and I always keep my watch five minutes ahead.

On Monday morning I awoke, lay abed in a sort of doze of relief and release. 'Is it true, is it really true,' I said to Victoria, 'that it's over at last? It's really over?' She told me it was true. 'And I don't have to go to the theatre, give notes, except when I want to?' She pointed out that I'd already undertaken to go in to the theatre twice during the coming week, and would presumably give notes. 'Yes, but I don't have to if I don't want to. That's the point. And I can lodge myself in Cell Block C and just pop in and out of the auditorium when I feel like it – but the process is over, there it is, on the stage, and I can … I can …' So I rambled excitedly on. Later, in the study to Sarah, I mentioned the telephone calls to Stephen while dismissing them as aberrations. I maintained my innocently babbling mode until Judy rang, to announce that she'd just heard from the Duncan Weldon organization that the advance was soaring, soaring, *Cell Mates* was a hit, a very big hit. I'd already known this, had said it to Victoria and Sarah, but it was delightful to have it from somebody over the telephone, because it somehow made it irreversible. I did wonder to Judy, though, why Duncan hadn't telephoned me himself, so that we could party together down the lines. She said, 'Oh, well, you know Duncan. Always somewhere else. At this moment he's probably tied up with Raquel Welch.' A bizarre image but, given the Duncan element, not an erotic one. He'd be busy hypnotizing the business into show business.

The rest of the morning passed in a flux of ruminations, some of them aloud to Sarah and Victoria, on the 'hit' theme, the Duncan-not-phoning theme, the looking-forward-to-Barbados theme, the back-in-the-black-at-the-bank theme, until Sarah reminded me that I was having lunch with Harold in five minutes' time – the Halcyon is three minutes away – and I'd better get my shoes on. Literally, as I never wear shoes around the house, even for company, and the ones I was using at the time, though comfortable, were extremely difficult to lace up, involving studs and loopings, etc., and would take up two of the five minutes I had to meet Harold in.

I had just completed this tiresome task when the phone rang. Sarah answered it as I stood up to make my little journey to the Halcyon. I waved at her to lie on my behalf – that I'd already left – unless it was in any way important – loved ones in trouble, compliments from God. It was in fact Duncan. The conversation went something like this:

ME: Hi, Duncan, how's everything going?
DUNCAN: Everything's fine at the box office. Busy all the time. I don't want to alarm you, but I've had one bit of strange news. Though I don't want to alarm you.

'I'm sorry. I'm so very sorry.' I heard those words, that tone echoing, before Duncan had finished his first sentences.

'It's Stephen,' he went on. 'He left a message on Lorraine Hamilton's answering machine –' Lorraine Hamilton being Stephen's agent – 'saying that there were some letters in his flat that he wanted her to pick up and deliver. She's done that. There was no sign of Stephen. But there's a letter for you, and one for Rik. The one for you is being biked around. It should get to you any minute.'

I trembled on the phone, Sarah exclaiming, 'What? What!' as she registered my expression, no doubt my complexion and my trembling. 'What's going on, what's going on?' I waved her to shut up, and asked Duncan if Lorraine Hamilton had also had a letter. Yes, he said, she had. And did it give any clue to his intentions? 'No, not really. Not where he's going, not what's happened to him, and no reason. She's very worried about him. Let's hope to God he hasn't done something dreadful to himself.'

The thought of Stephen, alone and in despair, dead in a ditch, in the Thames, standing on the ledge of a high building – 'I'm sorry. I'm so very sorry.' I think, crises to do with my family apart, it was the most ghastly moment of my life.

I told Duncan I'd give him the gist of Stephen's letter when I'd received it, until then I had no idea what to do. He said nor had he, 'God bless!' and hung up. I phoned Judy and told her about Duncan's call. Her first response was the classic 'You're joking!', which frequently means, 'This is terrible news that I believe utterly to be true, please don't deliver it.' I remembered lunch with Harold, his punctuality, that he'd been sitting waiting for some twenty minutes without a phone call of explanation, asked Sarah to get a message to him, and asked Victoria to accompany me to the Halcyon. During our walk we arranged that if the letter were to come while I was still with Harold, she would bring it up to me. When we entered the restaurant Harold was at a table in the far corner, by the window, beamingly eager to accept our apologies. Then he took in our expressions. Victoria left to await the letter, while Harold and I speculated, hypothesized, gnawed away at the imponderables – why? where? how? etc. – in a mainly circular fashion, as no sentence could lead anywhere but back to itself. After about an hour Victoria returned with the letter. I opened it with a desperate terror, a desperate hope. Were we looking towards funerals, memorial services to mark the end of a decent man's too short life, too highly successful career? Or would I see him on stage that night or the next, some time in the next few days, full of Stephen-like explanations and apologies – 'Oh, how silly of me, I don't know what got into me, just a sudden depression, how sweet you are, what darlings to forgive me, bless you' sort of thing?

The letter, as I read it, seemed to eliminate the second possibility, the hopeful one, comprehensively, without exactly completing the hideous threat of the first. A kind of, well, yes, *ambiguous* suicide letter, but difficult to interpret, though the balance seemed to be tilted towards suicide. But wherever he was going, whether to his untimely end, or into a hospital, or a monastery, or just into hiding, the letter made it unequivocally clear that a) he wasn't going to appear in *Cell Mates* again, indeed was never going to act again, and b) the reason for this was that he believed he was letting Rik, me and the whole production down. There was no reason, though, given to explain the reason, i.e. what made him think he was letting us all down, apart from a bizarre proclamation that he was personally responsible for 'any disappointments and inadequacies in the evening'. He followed this with a kind of spiteful lampoon on himself – 'the lumpen, superior "act" which I inflict on a bored audience every time I open my mouth'. This was clearly nonsense. Most actors would have forfeited cheques and even given them for the kind of tributes he'd been receiving and clearly enjoying for the last five weeks. And, as he didn't buy newspapers or read reviews …

We went through the letter a number of times, Victoria, Harold and I, rather like old-fashioned students parsing a piece of Latin, looking for clues to its real meaning, its real motive. Victoria left, Harold and I sat on and on, questioning, analysing, moving independently (or interdependently – conversations at times of crisis take a form of mutual, unconscious guidance) towards the view that he hadn't killed himself, and then away from it again. We both discounted the possibility of an emotional and nervous collapse. There was a fatalistic coherence about the letter that, in spite of its ambiguity, gave off a sense of declaration. Something darkly important, tragic and self-destructive had taken place. That is finally all we could make out of Stephen's letter.

I began to deal with the situation (but what situation?) by telephoning Lorraine Hamilton, Stephen's agent. From what she said, I gathered that her letter from Stephen didn't vary much from the one I'd received. He'd also written a lot of other letters, she said, that she'd also sent out. Why didn't I phone his sister and assistant, Jo, who wanted to talk to me? I phoned Jo – it was a turbulent, modern telephone-call business, involving all kinds of transfers from mobile to mobile – and finally succeeded in getting through to her. She was with her, with Stephen's, parents. She put her father, Stephen's father, on to the phone. He said in a gulping voice that Stephen's main problem was that, in spite of all his success, he had never learned to say 'no'. His agent, Lorraine Hamilton, had said much the same. But apparently, in all the letters heralding his ominous exit, he'd decided to say 'no' to everything, to a film script he was writing, a novel he'd contracted to, a starring role in *Cell Mates* – nothing but 'no's', here, there, everywhere. Like Lorraine Hamilton, Stephen's father had no idea where Stephen might be, but indicated in a grieving voice that he thought it was somewhere pretty distant – the other side of the Styx perhaps, seemed to be the shared but unspoken thought as we hung up.

I phoned up Duncan, as arranged and promised, only to discover that he was out, either to a late lunch, or an early lunch continuing late, or to tea, or an early dinner – so I spoke instead to Peter Wilkins, whose concerns were unlike anyone else's concerns so far. He wanted me to send over Stephen's letter, for their lawyer to have a look at. I refused, saying it was a personal letter, I couldn't see what lawyers had to do with the matter. He explained that Stephen might be in breach of contract – I couldn't really take it in – I mean, could you sue someone for committing suicide, was one of the thoughts that crossed my mind, for breaching their contract with life, or what? He asked me if the letter gave any explanation of the 'why' of his disappearance. After a bit of to-ing and fro-ing, I thought it wouldn't really be a breach on my own part, a breach of my personal code, to let him in on Stephen's vicious critique of himself as an actor, 'the lumpen, superior "act"' that bored an audience every time he opened his mouth. There was a pause at the end of the line, then something that sounded like a gasp.

WILKINS: But that's the *Financial Times* review.
ME: What?
WILKINS: Almost word for word. The *Financial Times* review.
ME: The *Financial Times*!

So there it was. Not Stephen on himself but the *Financial Times* on Stephen. A review I hadn't taken into consideration. A review I hadn't even, as far as I could remember, been warned about. But why should Stephen of all people be reading the *Financial Times*? A practising socialist, with no personal interest in money – he couldn't surely have been checking up on stocks and shares, the price of this or that commodity? No, there was no getting away from it. He had got hold of the *Financial Times* in search of a review of *Cell Mates*, a review of himself. A man who claimed that he took no notice of his reviews,didn't read newspapers as they were beneath contempt – yet he'd sloped out in the morning and bought himself the *Financial Times* ...

Peter Wilkins reverted to the matter of lawyers, then introduced the word 'insurance', his line being that if Stephen were alive and had simply walked out of the show because of a bad review, the management would have difficulty in collecting insurance. The insurance covered death, illness, but not betrayal. Those weren't his actual words, but that's what they amounted to. That the management had neglected to cover itself against a simple act of betrayal. Reasonable enough, I suppose, although I couldn't help reflecting that Stephen had been portraying on the stage a man to whom betrayal was routine, almost a reflex – and in his last performance had convinced the company manager that he'd finally mastered the part. So perhaps Stephen, in becoming a complete George Blake, had celebrated the achievement with a George Blake-like act of treachery. Or perhaps, as I reminded Peter Wilkins, he was dead. Destroyed by a world to which he'd over-committed himself. Peter Wilkins listened to all this with a kind of throbbing patience, and then reverted to his major topics: lawyers, insurance, what could be claimed back from Stephen out of Stephen's absence, if Stephen continued to maintain it, while failing to be maimed or dead.

There was nothing, I said, that we could do about Stephen. If he was dead we could grieve for him. If he was alive, we would have to wait upon his decision as to whether he had sufficient valour, spirit, morale to tough out the *Financial Times* review and put himself back on the stage. But his letter to me seemed pretty clear. One way or another he was gone, and, crude though it might seem, we had a living and highly successful production of a new play to protect. We had to think forwards, about a replacement, as well as backwards, in mourning – if mourning became the eventual claim on our emotions. 'Yes, well –' said

Peter Wilkins, we had to be careful, there was the insurance, there were the lawyers – supposing a year or two from now some smart lawyer claimed that a replacement amounted, at this early stage, to wrongful dismissal, and so we (he meant 'they', the management) couldn't claim the insurance. I asked him why, with a thriving play in the West End, with as big a star as Rik at the centre of it, they should even be *thinking* of lawyers and insurance; we should all be thinking replacement.

It went back and forth like this, he on his track to the future (lawyers, insurance, etc.), me on mine (get on with getting on with *Cell Mates*). We finally hung up having made only one clear decision: that nobody in the company should be made aware of the circumstances surrounding Stephen's departure – 'indisposed' would be the official story. Rik had already agreed to keep the contents of his letter from Stephen to himself until Stephen had had a chance to turn up again. Fat chance, I thought, fat chance that he'll turn up. At least on the stage of the Albery Theatre.

I began to feel – not with great clarity, but the feeling was there – that some die had been cast. That Duncan and Peter Wilkins were, possibly without knowing it themselves, already moving in a managerial way towards managerial ends (profit – or at least a curtailment of losses) whether *Cell Mates* lived or died. I kept returning to the two possibilities: the blacker of them was that Stephen was victim to himself; the other that *Cell Mates* would turn out to be Stephen's victim.

I arrived at the theatre well before 'the half' – the company is required to be in the theatre half an hour before curtain-up, hence the term 'the half' – and went straight to Rik's dressing room. 'Those fuckers,' he said, over and over. 'Those fuckers.' By which, of course, he meant the reviewers who had so deeply, possibly fatally, wounded Stephen. Though I clutched him as fiercely as he clutched me I couldn't completely share his emotions. 'No, that won't do, Rik,' I said. 'Actors, poets, playwrights, singers, directors are all liable to get bad reviews at many points in their careers – so are conductors, ballet dancers, chefs –' I didn't go on to say airline pilots and heart surgeons, theirs being less taxing jobs, carrying far less responsibility than the others, even if they do manage to make it to the newspapers from time to time, in an unfavourable light. But then again, I've never heard of a heart surgeon going off to commit suicide or whatever mid-operation, ditto an airline pilot in the middle of a flight. I actually did say a few things as loony as this, though not actually these things, because he was about to go on stage with the understudy, Mark Anderson, with whom he'd been rehearsing during the afternoon, and was emotionally devastated by the letter he'd received, which must have been more explicit than mine as his repeated references to the 'fuckers' who'd 'fucked' Stephen made clear, and so it seemed important to bring a bit of clarity and lightness into his dressing room. So we kept hugging, I kept aiming for jokes and common sense (and probably kept missing), kept berating 'the fuckers', whom I actually found myself defending – at least to the point of attempting to persuade him that most of them weren't homicidal psychopaths. So irony, laughter, jokes, let's take it easy, you're on stage with the understudy shortly, and you're going to be on stage with the understudy for quite a few performances, let's calm down here, was my inner director's approach. I told Rik I wouldn't stay for the performance. He said he didn't want me to, go home, think of what we're going to do next. 'We've got to survive this,' he said.

Then we went to Stephen's dressing room where Mark Anderson, the understudy, and the rest of the cast were waiting. I had to appear casual and jolly as I wished Mark luck and said no, I wasn't sure of the exact nature of Stephen's 'indisposition' – flu or something like that, I supposed. I was disgusting. At least I felt disgusting.

I loitered briefly at the back of the auditorium, where I had the pleasure of hearing David Bownes being greeted, during his announcement to the audience of Stephen's 'indisposition', by boos and hisses, thought of the actors similarly enjoying the experience on their Tannoys, then taxied back to w11, convinced – as Rik had shown by his ferocious display of emotion, of his sense of loss – that he too was convinced that Stephen wasn't coming back.

'What to do next' was obvious. To find a replacement before the management, the lawyers, the insurance brokers, moved in and made completely other decisions. I couldn't keep my mind away from the telephone conversation with Peter Wilkins – do something quickly, I thought, replace Stephen immediately. But how, with whom?

That night there was a phone call from David Bownes who of course knew the true situation. He said that Mark had grown in confidence from scene to scene, Rik had been marvellous with him, but off stage, in the privacy of his dressing room, Rik had been distraught, in tears of grief, tears of anger. He also mentioned what I already knew, that he'd been booed and hissed when making the announcement about Stephen – but he didn't mind, not at all, it was part of his job. I didn't really think it could be part of anybody's job to be booed and hissed by a full house. It was the 'kill the messenger' syndrome. We had to do everything possible to stop David Bownes being killed, night after night.

Later, in my study, listening to Mozart, drinking champagne, smoking, I sat at my desk in a kind of coma, from shock. A play that had been a triumph on Saturday night, an established success by Sunday, with a soaring box office on Monday morning, was by Monday night in a state of crisis, with a potential, or already achieved, death at its centre.

The next morning I had a small inspiration. I phoned Stephen's sister, Jo, and said that if Stephen was OK, not dead but had merely done a bunk, the best solution, indeed the only solution, from his and the company's point of view, from Rik's point of view, his family's point of view, was for Stephen to get himself into a clinic as quickly as possible, claiming (perhaps truthfully) that he was in severe emotional distress and needed treatment. She said yes, she could see the point of that, but so far he hadn't been in touch with her, or his parents, with anybody as far as she knew. She did say, though, that in his letter to her he'd instructed her to make sure his Barclaycard was in credit, as he'd need it, and that Stephen's bank manager, who was a close friend of Stephen's – which shows that some bank managers know their business – had told her that Stephen had spent large sums of money on whisky and cigarettes, and on a lot of books. So if he'd planned to commit suicide, it was by smoking, drinking and reading himself to death. But why did he need the Barclaycard? Perhaps Stephen, worldly in so many ways, knows something about the cost of getting up to heaven that the rest of us don't. I entertained a brief fantasy of Stephen greeting St Peter with his credit card and expecting – with a smile as benign as St Peter's, treating St Peter as the maître d', so to speak, and anticipating the usual service – the best table, immediate waiters (St this and St that) – 'No, no fuss. Bless you!' But then imagining St Peter relieving him of his Barclaycard, gently referring him to somewhere where the service would be of a very different and distinctly lower order. I slid fondly back into the evening after rehearsal when we'd developed the theme of the critic ascending to heaven. An anguished spasm of nostalgia – ah, those were the days kind of stuff.

I shook back into the practical world by phoning Lorraine Hamilton and repeating the advice I'd given to Stephen's sister, that if Stephen got in touch, she should advise him to get straight into a clinic, have himself diagnosed as being in the throes of a nervous breakdown, the consequence of overwork, etc. She'd obviously come to much the same conclusion. But as Stephen hadn't been in touch, and as she hadn't the slightest idea where he was, there was nothing she could do at the moment but wait. Like the rest of us.

Then either Peter Wilkins or Duncan himself – I can't remember which – phoned to ask if I had any news. I reported on my conversation with Stephen's sister and with his agent. Whoever was on the end of the management's line became quite enthusiastic at the thought of Stephen in a clinic, presumably both for legal and insurance reasons and from concern for Stephen himself. I asked how the 'quotes' were going, had they got any outside the theatre yet? He said they were working on it, these things took time. And they'd need to put up some for Stephen, if Stephen came back. It may have been then that I bellowed, 'He's not coming back! Don't you understand! He has no intention of coming back. Whether alive or dead – Rik and I, who know him far better than you do, know that he's not coming back!' He said yes, but from the legal point of view, with the insurance to consider – I didn't actually hang up on Duncan or Peter Wilkins, whichever it was, as I've taught myself never to hang up on people, but I certainly didn't think it was a conversation worth prolonging. It must have been then, Tuesday, that I postponed the flight to Barbados, and persuaded the hotel to allow us to keep the deposit (a substantial one) open for a stay in the, I hoped, near future.

Later that day, after a few people had phoned to commiserate – friends to whom I hadn't broken the news, so the story was already rippling around town – Sarah suddenly remarked that our mutual friend, that fine actor, Simon Ward, would be finishing his long stint in *On Approval* at the end of the week, what did I think? I thought for not very long. I phoned Simon and sounded him out, explaining that it had to be a confidential conversation, nothing might come of it, Stephen might, just might, reappear, and of course I'd have to talk to the management, but would he be interested? Yes, he said. Very. Coincidentally he had arranged to go to the matinée of *Cell Mates* the next day, Wednesday, his own matinée being on a Thursday. I said I'd get back to him, phoned the management, got Peter Wilkins. Yes, he said, yes, Simon was a wonderful idea, an actor he admired enormously. He sounded quite uplifted until he abruptly downlifted himself – hang on a minute, hang on a minute, weren't we rushing it? His lawyer had advised the Weldon organization that it would be 'legally wise' (can those two words ever be in juxtaposition?) to give Stephen time to return, there were certain steps that had to be taken: first, a letter to Stephen's agent, noting that he'd failed to appear on the stage on Monday and Tuesday, assumed he was 'indisposed', hoped he was on his way to a swift recovery; then, when Stephen failed to turn up for the next performance without explanation, another letter indicating that he was potentially in breach of contract; and then, after a further absence without explanation, a third letter declaring that Stephen was now actually in breach of contract, and would have to be replaced. These three stages, Peter Wilkins said, had to be gone through, according to their lawyer – otherwise the hypothetical defence lawyer of the future could go on the attack by suing the management for Stephen's wrongful dismissal, rather than having the management's case for breach of contract pass uncontested. And where would the management be then, especially in relation to insurance? I became quite forceful – rowdy, in fact – asserting yet again that Stephen wouldn't be coming back, every performance he missed making it more impossible for him; that Rik might be close to leaving the show (and who could blame him?) because, from back-stage reports, he was becoming more, not less, distressed – he needed, not an understudy, however good the understudy was as an understudy, but an authoritative and established Blake, he deserved it, furthermore, and furthermore and furthermore.

There were a lot of furthermores that included a demand that David Bownes should never again have to be booed and hissed at before the evening had begun – it was painful for all, most particularly for David Bownes. He said there *was* a notice in the lobby, though he admitted it was a small one, to the side of the box office, a notice that the incoming audience might not notice, he'd see to it that a larger one was put somewhere, so that there'd be no need for David Bownes to make any announcement whatsoever. To one of my other furthermores – that there were still no quotes outside the theatre – he said they were working on it, there should be something up later in the day. Now, I said, on the question of Simon Ward – to which he replied, 'Well, if only we had some hard evidence that Stephen's not coming back. And that it's his decision.' 'But you don't understand,' I said. 'You really don't!' And went through it all again, even more rhetorically, even more loudly, than before. Yes, yes, Peter Wilkins said, he understood what I was saying but if I could just bring myself to fax a copy of Stephen's letter for the lawyers to look at – I finally accepted that Stephen's letter to me would have to pass into the management's hands, and faxed it through. Later, Peter Wilkins phoned to say that in the lawyer's opinion Stephen's letter stated unequivocally that he'd left the production deliberately, and made it clear that he had no intention, under any circumstances, of returning. So we could go ahead with Simon Ward.

I had an absolute horror of going into the theatre, as I couldn't face telling further lies to the cast and stage management, but I must have popped in furtively to see Rik, because I have two very vivid memories of him in his dressing room, of his saying that the understudy had been fine, 'But Stevie, I miss my Stevie', and I can still see his face as he said it. The other memory – Rik lying on the sofa, staring at me with a kind of snarl. 'He hasn't killed himself. Not Stephen. I *know* Stephen. He'd never do it.' Yes, he knew Stephen, his Stevie, full of erudition but always full of sweetness and, for Rik's talents, full of almost doting admiration. Rik was so certain, so angry and contemptuous and certain, that I believed him instantly. He hadn't worked it out, he'd just seen a fundamental truth about Stephen. I know these two moments happened on the same evening, before the half, the missing of Stephen and the snarling dismissal of the possibility that he might have committed suicide, with only a short space in between.

That night I sat on in my study, listening to Bach, Beethoven, Mozart, waiting for the comatose drifting, the one that guarantees sleep. It still hadn't begun its leisurely and soothing crawl through my body and my consciousness when the phone rang. It was one in the morning and it was Duncan. He said he'd only just got home, been busy all day and most of the night sorting out something (not to do with *Cell Mates*)t, sorry he hadn't returned my call. I couldn't think what call he hadn't returned, then remembered that I always automatically and out of courtesy asked for Duncan before being passed on to Peter Wilkins – Duncan being the roast-beef-eating chappie, so to speak, and Peter Wilkins being the two other chappies, simultaneously going to market and staying at home – or at least at the office. I couldn't think of anything I hadn't already said to Peter Wilkins that I could say to Duncan, but I said it all again anyway, until once again I found myself bellowing something along the lines that the insurance didn't matter, the lawyers didn't matter, what *did* matter was the survival of *Cell Mates*. He went through a little passage of aggressive agreement – 'Yes, yes, that's the important thing,' he said, '*Cell Mates*, that's the important thing!' I told him about Simon Ward, my conversation with him. He said he already knew about it; that's why he was phoning really. His own position was that, oh yes, he was a great admirer of Simon Ward, but how did we go about it? I said, 'Let's accept the fact that Stephen's left, issue a press release to that effect, giving out the reasons he's given to Rik, to me, to his sister Jo, to his agent Lorraine, to his family, to various friends, including probably his bank manager for all we knew. The story is already all over London, he's written too many letters for us to do anything but tell the truth, the truth is on its way out, and it might do the production less damage if it came from us, direct, in a press release, rather than built itself through rumour, gossip, speculation'. There was a pause, during which I thought insurance agents and lawyers were about to surface. Instead, Duncan said, 'I'm all for Simon Ward. But the press release – *you* should do it.' 'Me! Why me? You're the management, the production company.' 'Yes,' he said, 'but you're the writer, the professional writer. You'd do it better than we would. Telling the truth of it all.' 'But what about your PR guy, this is his sort of job, what he's employed to do?' 'Ah, but the PR guy is in Australia at the moment, holidaying, isn't really in touch with the situation except by telephone or by fax, won't be in London for over a week' – thus leaving me, the professional writer, to do his job for him. After all, he pointed out, the PR guy wasn't to know that Stephen was going to do a bunk, commit suicide, whatever Stephen had done. I was the professional writer, so do my task. And then we could get on with the business in hand, which was signing up Simon Ward, who would do us all proud, God bless.

It took me until four in the morning to write a brief press release to the effect that Stephen was a man 'in emotional disarray'. I gave a précis of the explanation that he'd offered in his letter. The next morning Sarah faxed the release through to Duncan's office, where someone – Duncan and/or Peter Wilkins – gave it the nod, and sent it out, along with – for reasons I still can't understand – a statement of their own saying simply that Stephen had left the production 'for personal reasons'. I mean, why get me to issue a statement on the grounds that I'm the professional writer if they intended to issue one themselves, one that didn't so much contradict mine as evade it? 'Personal reasons' are almost completely meaningless, as most, if not all, motives for human behaviour are in some way or another 'personal', and the public use of the phrase could give rise to endless speculation – that he and Rik had come to fisticuffs in the dressing room, that he'd run away with his bank manager, that there was no decent food to be found in the neighbourhood, that he'd bought a dog and had to take it to Norfolk to house-train it – while there, in my statement, was a clear definition of Stephen's 'personal reasons' as provided by the ultimate authority, his own person. I couldn't make out what the management, in the shape of Duncan and/or Peter Wilkins, could possibly be up to.

I phoned Simon Ward and told him he was on, if he wanted to be. He said he was pretty sure he did. I arranged with David Bownes to meet him in the foyer, to give him an up-to-date version of the script, with all the moves and new lines in, then phoned Rik and told him what was taking place. He didn't know Simon's work, he said, but knew of his reputation as a serious and proper actor, he was relieved that *something* was being done, let's for God's sake get on with it.

At some point during the day Harold phoned to say that it might sound impertinent, but shouldn't I go in, see the show, shake the understudy by the hand. I explained that I couldn't go back-stage, not until we had a *situation nette,* as no offer had yet been officially made to Simon, who therefore wasn't officially cast, and I couldn't face any of the actors except Rik until I could tell them the truth, that Stephen was gone, Simon was in. That of course I'd honour the understudy, but not while he was Stephen's understudy, only when he was Simon's understudy

and filling in for Simon while Simon was rehearsing. I couldn't –
just couldn't – do all the lying about Stephen, not again, once
was enough. 'Ah! Well, I hadn't really grasped the problem,'
Harold said. 'But I think,' he added, 'that Simon Ward will make
a very good Blake. An excellent Blake. He's a fine actor. I hope
he does it.'

I sat in my study with fingers crossed, clutching wood, waiting for Simon to phone, after the matinée. He did. He liked the
play very much, very much wanted to play Blake, intended to
spend the rest of the evening, before and after his performance,
studying the script. David Bownes had taken him back-stage to
meet Rik, whom he'd liked immediately. Then David Bownes
phoned, to say how delighted Rik had been with Simon, they'd
got on famously. I then phoned the management, got Peter
Wilkins, as usual, and reported that Simon wanted to do the
play, Rik liked him and wanted him to do it, that I wanted him
to do it – could we please proceed? He said, yes, we could, reaf-
firmed his faith in Simon, didn't mention lawyers or insurance.
So back to Simon, to declare that the management had given the
go-ahead, negotiations would probably take a few days, but
would he – I drew a breath – consider starting rehearsals with
the understudies tomorrow, to learn the moves, get the lines
under his belt? 'Of course,' he said. 'The sooner the better.' So
back to David Bownes, to arrange the understudy rehearsal for
Simon, and that was the day, Wednesday, when Blake, the part
of Blake, moved definitively from Stephen Fry, who had been
playing it for over a month, to Simon Ward, who had only just
received the script and seen one performance. I was exhausted.
Exhausted and relieved.

As I recall it, I went in to the theatre in the evening, up to Cell
Block C, in which Duncan and Peter Wilkins were already waiting. I said to them, assuming that they already realized it, that
Stephen's vanishing was going to be a big story – 'A very big
story. Which will almost certainly harm the play.' Duncan then
said the second most inaccurate thing anyone has ever said to
me – that he didn't think the media would be particularly interested, one of the tabloids might pick it up, and it might make the

back page of the *Guardian*. Whereupon Peter Wilkins said the most inaccurate thing anyone has ever said to me, which was, 'There's no such thing as bad publicity. The more the better.'

PART IV

Thursday morning didn't mean much to me, rings no bells in retrospect, until I clambered into a taxi and had myself driven off to the Albery, to show support for Simon and to put to him a plan of action. I watched him learning his lines and moves for a while from a seat in the stalls. I was astonished at the speed with which he was working, the good-natured ferocity of his concentration, berating himself whenever he got a line wrong. During a break, he came and sat beside me. He apologized for not being able to stay past midday, but he had to hustle himself off to rehearse with the understudies for *On Approval*, as his leading lady (Anna Carteret, Christopher Morahan's wife) had fallen ill. And then there was the matinée, then the evening performance. That was his day. Rehearsing with understudies as he tried to learn a new play; rehearsing with the understudies of the play he was in; then a matinée; then an evening performance. He was anxious to assure me that he'd be able to do a full day's rehearsal tomorrow – and then the next day, Saturday, *On Approval* would close, he'd come around to my place on Sunday to go through the text. I'd come in on Monday and Tuesday for proper rehearsal with the actual cast, I said, and then – attempting casual matter-of-factness – 'I'd like to put you in on Wednesday.' 'Wednesday?' He looked mildly concerned, though the mildness probably concealed a deep concern, if not panic itself. Well, why not panic? 'I know it's a bit rushed,' I said, and explained about Rik, who would by then have done ten performances with the understudy, was still in emotional shock at losing Stephen, both as his friend and his Blake, and needed a full-time, authoritative partner on stage with him.

91

Otherwise things might fall apart. 'Yes, Rik's a very emotional man, isn't he? I mean, I'd always assumed, from seeing him on television, that he'd be – well, cocky, robust, taking things as they come or forcing them along, but when I went round to his dressing room, I could see he's not like that at all.' 'A very emotional man,' I said. 'And a very generous one. You'll find that on stage he'll play straight to you, he'll give and give and give. With his eyes, with his feelings. You'll know exactly where he is dramatically every second you're together – you'll know where you have to be every second.' Simon pondered this. Having been on stage with quite a few actors who gave him nothing, indeed tried to take things away from him by looking anywhere but towards him, preferring on the whole to look towards the audience instead, he appreciated the point. 'Look, I'll *try* for Wednesday night,' he said, 'but I don't want to go through rehearsals knowing I *have* to be ready by then. It might mess up my concentration.' I made it clear that he would on no account be thrust, bullied, harassed or blackmailed on to the stage in front of a West End audience until he was ready; Wednesday night wasn't a deadline, it was a target. Actually I'd already set another target – Wednesday matinée – for him, but thought it inadvisable to mention this. Still, I'd have taken bets that Simon would certainly be up on the boards on Wednesday night at the latest, giving stuff back to Rik that Rik badly needed.

I went around to the front of the house, to check whether the management had managed to get some quotes up. There were a few, a very few, and not ones that I'd expected. Instead of 'A masterful comedy, fine new play' or 'I spy a triumph' or 'I spy a fine tale of treachery and friendship', all of which were available from national newspapers, we had on offer words like 'fascinating' and 'engrossing', which, while not actually lethal, didn't make the pulse-rate rise, the hand reach for its credit card. The line from the *Sunday Telegraph* omitted the two key words, which were 'highly entertaining', so that what was left had been emasculated into dreary respectability. But none of this mattered very much, because in order to read what there was to read and wasn't worth reading anyway, you had to step around an enormous and funereal placard, announcing that Stephen Fry was no longer appearing in the production. That was it, the main, the only significant quote, so to speak, framed like news of a death. And all around, everywhere you looked, were posters of Rik and Stephen. Very sombre posters, the idea for which I'd proposed myself. I don't believe I've ever seen in my life such a gloomy front of house. It seemed to be inviting the public to pay tribute to a corpse, a corpse with an unsuccessful life behind it, at that.

In the taxi on the way home I passed *Evening Standard* hoardings, which proclaimed that 'Fears grow for Stephen Fry'. The hoardings seemed like a sinister confirmation of the large, black placard outside the theatre, the narrative run backwards, so to speak, the death announced at the Albery, and the fears for life announced all over London – but no longer, in my mind, to do with Stephen, but with the production of *Cell Mates*. 'Fears grow for *Cell Mates*' and '*Cell Mates* is no longer appearing at this theatre' is what I read inwardly, where Stephen had begun to assume the twin roles of assassin and undertaker. This is what is called, I think, prescience. But hope, wretched hope, springs eternal, an agent of the devil that fills the graveyards with those spiritually and physically exhausted by it. So I went on hoping. What else was there to do? The important thing, I thought, as the taxi ploughed and stuttered past the *Standard* hoardings – once actually stalling in traffic next to one – the important thing is to rid ourselves of Stephen, get him out of our emotions and memories. At least until the show was flowing along again.

I got straight on the wire to Peter Wilkins. I'd discovered that there was no point in *showing* anger to him – keep it down below the surface, for the cultivation of my ulcers, because, like me, he met anger with bluster, which then made for bluster from me and anger from him. I began by telling him how well Simon was already fitting in, how impressed the stage management was by his alertness, concentrated quickness, his feeling for the part. The real subject I smoothed into. 'Now, about the front of house, Peter –' and then I described what I'd seen and what effect it had had on me. On the question of the Stephen-Fry-being-absent placard, he replied that I myself had demanded it, in order to spare David Bownes his pre-performance hisses and boos. I said there was a difference between a notice and a Mediterranean-sized tombstone, besides which it would be more to the point to celebrate Simon Ward's entry into the company. He said, 'Now hold on a minute. We haven't finished contracting Simon yet. And what about the Trade Descriptions Act?' 'The Trade Descriptions Act!' I yelped, anger showing and thus my ulcer going unfed, 'What the fuck do you mean!' 'Well,' said Peter Wilkins, 'if people come to the theatre expecting Stephen Fry and they get an understudy, without our having announced they'll be getting an understudy, we could be liable. Under the Trade Descriptions Act.' 'Oh, come on,' I said. 'There isn't a person in the country who doesn't know that Stephen has gone. It's been front-page news in the press, it's been on television, on the radio. And this is a theatre-going audience we're talking about. Do you think they don't read the papers, watch the television news, listen to the radio. They only knew the play was on because of the blanket coverage. Which is why they now think the play's off. Because of blanket coverage about Stephen.' He argued that all we knew at this stage about Stephen was what had so far been made public – i.e. that he'd gone out on the Sunday evening (at 5.40?) to do a scheduled reading of *Peter and the Wolf*, which he apparently delivered sitting down instead of, as is the convention, on his feet. He was described by one of the musicians – so it was reported – as looking decidedly withdrawn, and had refused to attend the party afterwards on the grounds that he had to be up early. And that was all we knew.

Yes, I said, yes, yes, yes, I know all that, I've read some of it myself, but he's gone, we all finally agree that he's gone, and Simon Ward is taking over. Peter Wilkins conceded the point. Stephen's name would come out of the ads and the posters, Simon's name would go up in his place, Simon would be coming in soon, as a permanent (we hoped) feature, Stephen gone and forgotten. On to the matter of the quotes. 'These things take time,' he said, yet again. 'To choose them, to get them on to placards – ten days at least.' I was instantly back in my bellowing mode. 'But this is an emergency! Don't you understand? An emergency! Unless we act quickly – quickly – quickly – unless we present ourselves proudly to the world, with Rik Mayall, with no need for Stephen Fry, we'll be down the tubes. Over and done with.' He remained obdurately and blusteringly calm. He'd see what he could do, couldn't promise, they went about things in their own way, the people who put quotes up outside the theatre. He said he would do his best to chivvy them along, these people (whose well-remunerated task in life was simply to assemble a large clutch of quotes and post them outside the playhouse).

On this note we ended. What note? I couldn't help feeling that there were more kinds of retreats going on than just Stephen's. Nobody who cared about the production's future could have allowed the current display outside the Albery. Every visual signal was 'Don't come and see me. Don't buy a ticket. We're finished.' I wasn't as lucid as this at the time, if this is lucid, but the apprehensions were like sharks in my system. I have strong feelings about sharks, believing that every single one of them, unless they can prove, with heavy documentation, that they are by nature benefactors and pets, should be exterminated. But sharks, lawyers, insurance investigators, producers, seemed to be moving with canny purpose towards a dangling, vulnerable, almost nude play. A snap of the limb here, a limb there, a delve at the torso, a rip at the groin. In other words, the play had long ceased to be 'the thing'. It was only 'the thing' when it might guarantee a return on investment. When that was in danger, look at, snap at the play, gorge on all the loss-assuaging options, to hell with five years of writing, three months of production, snap, snap, snap. Gorge, gorge, gorge. Teeth and snouts, dangling limbs and tempting torsos. And on to the next. Raquel Welch. Even, who knows, Clint Eastwood as Hamlet. On to the next. And from their point of view, why not? That was 'the business' they were in.

As for me, as for Rik, as for the rest of the company, it was on to the next day, in our struggle to keep the organism alive. Our organism. The advances were still very good, people having bought their tickets in advance, without any advance knowledge of the disaster that had befallen the company, and therefore having to endure the replacement of Stephen with a completely unheard-of understudy whose work – extremely competent work – they invariably ended up applauding, as they invariably applauded the whole show, and especially Rik, whose domination of the stage they adored. But as the story of Stephen's defection – abdication – betrayal – whatever – grew and grew, the audiences began to dwindle. On Friday, there was a paltry and mournful notice outside the theatre announcing at last that the part previously played by Stephen Fry was shortly to be played by Simon Ward.

It was either that night or the next evening that I went up to Cell Block C, in which Duncan and Peter Wilkins eventually joined me. Along with Rik's agent, Aude Powell. I had Victoria as my companion-in-arms. There was an odd air of jocularity in Cell Block C. We'd all observed the diminished house, but still, there it was, the jocularity. We stood about with glasses of champagne in our hands, cigarettes between these fingers, cigars between those, talking and laughing about nothing in particular, until somebody, either Duncan or Peter Wilkins, made a comment about Stephen's being spotted on a cross-Channel ferry – he'd given out autographs in, one gathers, his ever-generous and charming way to English fellow passengers, as he headed towards Bruges. 'What!' I shouted. 'He's in Bruges! Are you saying he's in Bruges! What the fuck is he doing in Bruges?'

Apparently, Stephen's father had appeared on some television news programme to explain why his offspring was currently in Bruges instead of on the West End stage, where he'd contracted to be. 'Yes,' Stephen's father had said. 'Why not Bruges? A beautiful city. If I were Stephen –' (i.e. if I were my son) – 'that's where I'd head for in his sort of situation. And the first thing I'd find out about was the restaurants – where there was a decent restaurant.' Or words to that effect. On television. On the news. On the main news came the news that the genetic theory was correct, that both father and son would flee to Bruges – no, not flee, but kind of elope with those darlings of their hearts – their stomachs – when in a psychic pickle. Like son, like father. And vice versa. And versa vice. *Quels hommes!*

I was beside myself. I mean that almost literally. There was somebody standing right beside myself who was in fact me, who kept shouting, 'Bruges, Bruges, how can the bugger be in Bruges! *Why* should the bugger be in Bruges!' Nobody could offer, except the father who'd already offered it, a reasonable explanation: a beautiful city, fine restaurants. And lots of Belgians who shared Stephen's appetites which would make him feel that he was in congenial company, I suppose. Dining in his gastric peer group. I made an enraged peroration along these lines – clearly unfair to Stephen's father, who was attempting to cope publicly with a private bewilderment, and possibly unfair to Stephen, who might, for all I knew, have gone to Bruges for its spiritual sustinence – its cathedral, say, its small religious sanctuaries.

PART V

It won't be a big story, Duncan had said. Anyway, there's no such thing, Peter Wilkins had said, as bad publicity.

Most news stories explode, hang about for a few days, dwindle, die. This one found ways of exploding day after day, week after week, splashing all over the newspapers, on the radio, on television. When any attention was given to *Cell Mates* it was derisory. The main press account delivered by reporters who'd clearly neither seen the play nor read the reviews, even in their own newspapers, was that Stephen had left the play and the production because the play and the production had received bad reviews. The *Standard* chappie appeared on television news and rubbished the play, and the production. Millions of people were therefore told as a hard fact – just as four people killed in an accident on the M4, a bomb going off in Kentish Town, a newsagent shot in Shepherd's Bush, England had just lost a cricket/soccer/rugby international are hard facts – that the play was no good and that Stephen had left because of it. Hard fact. The *Guardian*, ever vigilant in its defence of truth and the decencies, published an article quoting the unfavourable reviews, neglecting to mention that the *Guardian*'s own reviewer had written both warmly and intelligently about the play. The Standard, which behaved as Rotweilers are sometimes said to behave with children, mauled us again and again, in this column and that. On and on and on it went, not just in the *Standard* but in all the other newspapers, across the world – Australia, Canada, the States – variations on the same story, that Stephen had fled from a disaster. Stephen had become a martyr to the misfortune of myself, my writing, my directing.

I issued two further press releases, which, I hoped, would stem or redirect this relentless torrent. My first was intended to be an ironic but relieved celebration, after the announcement of Stephen's continuing existence – 'now that we know that Stephen Fry is alive and well and dining in Bruges' – and went on to point out that Rik Mayall was about to be joined by Simon Ward in *Cell Mates*. This turned out to be a futile, because generally unnoticed, effort. I received a second letter from Stephen, postmarked Innsbruck, in which he confessed that he'd 'slunk' away in the most 'cowardly' fashion, 'out of the kitchen' because he 'couldn't stand the heat', how ashamed he was of what he'd done, of the distress he'd caused to Rik, myself, the rest of the cast, how inadequate he felt as an actor and as a moral being – and so forth. He also said that he'd actually listened to my message in response to his 'Sorry. So very sorry' while in the bathroom, contemplating his sleeping pills. Whether he was still there for my second phone call he didn't say. He followed this with a press release faxed from Bruges, or Eastern Europe, or the South of France, wherever he happened to be holing up at the time – in the South of France he was seen in a hamlet, wearing a beret and calling himself Monsieur Simon, whether in deference to me or to Simon Ward I can't determine, but when I first had this reported to me I mistook the meaning, thinking that he was appearing as an actor in *Hamlet* under the pseudonym of Monsieur Simon – 'But what part, what part could he possibly play? Polonius? Osric? Yes, Osric makes a lot of sense –' until it was explained that the hamlet he'd been seen in was a small village, and that Monsieur Simon wasn't a stage name, it was how he passed himself off as he went about his business phoning on his mobile, sending faxes, making dates in his speak-back diary for late 1995, 1996 – that sort of thing, I suppose. At least that's how I – probably unfairly – imagined him. Anyway, from wherever he was in the world, he delivered a long, clarifying and completely decent public statement that he'd left *Cell Mates* because he felt he was a failure as an actor, wasn't good enough for the part of Blake, was letting down Rik and the rest of the cast on stage, knew that Simon Ward would bring more to the play than he ever could. In fact, he publicly and honestly restated what he'd already stated to Rik, myself and so many other people in private letters. Even when he had this statement published in every newspaper in the country, paraphrased on television and radio, the simple truth of the matter, it was ignored. It was comprehensively ignored. It was the play's fault, the playwright-director's fault – the same theme, again and again.

I issued my final press statement, previously and over-fondly described as 'foolish'. Looking at it again, I realize with a shudder that it was far worse than that – both homicidal and suicidal, the unnatural conception of those two turbulent bedmates, rage and hurt. A brutishly unfair attack on Stephen's abilities as an actor followed by an over-moralizing outrage at his subsequent behaviour. My sane intention, if I was at the moment of its release in any way sane, was once again to direct attention back to the play, to Rik and to Simon. My achievement was to direct even more attention to Stephen, whom I'd not only martyred and victimized in my role as playwright/director but was now assisting towards canonization in my newly discovered role as public relations expert.

I pursued this new role with my usual aplomb. I allowed a London television news programme to film me through a window of the house I live in, as I bent academically over what was purported to be the script of *Cell Mates* but was in fact a script of Harold's *Old Times* (I couldn't find a copy of *Cell Mates*, *Old Times* was the most script-looking script to hand). They questioned me, not unsympathetically, and at some length but to no real purpose, as what finally appeared on the screen was a sound-bite and a sight-bite that somehow blinked the play into the past. I did a couple of early-morning radio interviews on the telephone, cursing Stephen (though not out loud on the airwaves) for my having a glass of champagne and a cigarette on the go at an hour when I am usually unconscious and therefore abstinent. I also dealt with a blank-voiced woman from the *Independent* who phoned up to challenge my sensitivity and integrity in wanting the play to go on, given that I'd said in my first release that Stephen must be in 'emotional disarray'. I replied suavely that when I'd written that I thought he might be dead, slain by his own hand, or rambling about the motorways, miming his part, speechless and mad; I hadn't realized that he was in Bruges, and with enough speech at his command – and in a foreign tongue at that – to order himself meals. 'Oh, come on,' she said. 'Oh, come on,' came this almost psychopathically blank voice. 'Don't you care about him, about what's happened to him, what you've done to him?' 'Oh, you mean the *Financial Times* review? I did that to him, did I?' She declared inevitably that the play itself had received bad reviews. I asked her if she'd read through them. No, she said, but she'd read about their being bad, seen it on television. 'Have you read your own reviewer's reviews?' I asked, mentioning that he'd actually reviewed it twice, the first time calling it 'a masterly comedy', the second 'a fine new play'. There was a pause, not a pause of embarrassment but the pause of sheer inattentiveness, as if my questions were bumble bees and that she was waiting for them to depart through the window and out of her concerns. 'Stephen Fry's suffering,' she said. 'That poor man is suffering, and you abuse him in a press release. I can't see why you're being so hard on him. So cruel. Think of the suffering he's going through –'

The Times, on the other hand, managed to damage *Cell Mates* without any intervention on my part. The paper's lead reviewer had written a favourable account of the play and the production, extracts from which would look well on the placards. It was something of a surprise then to discover in the lavatory a second review in *The Times* contradicting everything the previous reviewer had said. He began his piece with a pointed reference to the sparsity of the house, stitched in sneering dismissals of Simon Ward – who had at this stage given only four performances – and concluded by congratulating Stephen on his departure, finding fault with him only for not having done it earlier, at the first read-through in fact.

It was shortly after I'd been bitten publicly (though while on the lavatory) by *The Times* that the private hate mail began to arrive at the stage door, some of it delivered by hand. It seemed mainly to have been written by elderly spinsters in spasms of exalted spite, pretty well what you'd expect from elderly and maiden Stephen Fry groupies, lurking out there in the shrubberies, secateurs in one hand, something from the garden dying or dead in the other.

Actually I picked up what was probably my first piece of hate mail on the evening that Stephen had been signing autographs on his way to Bruges, but I can't be sure, as I wasn't allowed to read it. Rik, Aude Powell, Victoria and I went on after the show, which had played to a decent house – we were still living on our advance – to the Ivy. I had a little pile of unopened post on the table in front of me. Rik picked up this pile, sorted rapidly through it, not opening anything, but with a strange physical concentration, running his hands over the envelopes, as if sucking the contents up through his fingers. He extracted one letter from the pile, passed it on to Aude, passed the rest back to me. 'Hey, what's going on?' I said. 'Isn't that my letter – I mean, it's to me, isn't it?' 'You don't want to read it,' Rik said. 'No, you don't want to read it,' Aude said. 'But how do you know?' By this time the letter had completely vanished, having been torn up and stuffed somewhere by Aude. 'Are you familiar with the handwriting, is that it?' No, Aude said, but Rik had a second or seventh sense, whichever sense is required for the detection of hate mail, and that I was to trust him. 'Trust me,' Rik said. 'You won't want to read that letter.' It made no difference whether I trusted him or not, as the letter was no longer available to be read, unless I were to insist on having it back and pasting its fragments together for the sole purpose of being abused. The fact is, I did trust Rik, in all his instincts, and knew he'd be right about the letter, now dispatched by Rik through Aude to oblivion.

Actually that evening passed in a state of crazed joy. The thought of Stephen in Bruges somehow set the four of us alight, in spite of the misery the fact of his being there caused us all – Stephen included probably. We drew verbal pictures of Bruges – none of us had ever visited it – with Stephen in it, attempting to pass himself off as a native of the city (he'd been sighted wearing a beret), playing with his technological toys in his comfortable hotel room or doing a studious circuit of the best restaurants. By the time we were in our taxi, heading westward, we were helpless with laughter, life-threatening laughter that caused the driver to sit stiffly, clenched, as if afraid to turn and confront the fact that he had a quartet of uncontrollable lunatics or drunks – we weren't drunk, except on jokes – rocking about in the back. In retrospect it seems to have been posthumous – rather than gallows – humour, inspired by the sense we all shared of impending calamity. Still, joyous nights out are joyous nights out, snap them up whenever you can, whatever the circumstances that lead up to them, whatever the prospects ahead.

Come Monday midday there I was, stuck in the stalls of the Albery Theatre yet again, directing Simon Ward, Rik Mayall and the cast of *Cell Mates*. It would have been a completely exhilarating experience, Simon being so quick to respond, Rik being so eagerly responsive to the complicated variations Simon brought to his Blake, if it hadn't had to be so rushed. I also got sick of the sound of my own voice, as I gesticulated there, pointed there, commanded to there – my voice, my voice, three and a half months of this voice.

The next day, Tuesday, we worked demonically. Simon was learning, getting himself into the part, discovering the joys of playing with Rik's spontaneity. Rik was exhausted, emotionally wrung out by the events of the last week, but enjoying every minute of his intercommunication with Simon. After rehearsals, in what had been Stephen's dressing room and was now Simon's, I unveiled my master plan: that Simon should go into the play, not the next evening, for which he was clearly underprepared, but the next afternoon, when he would be even less prepared. Simon looked extremely tense as I put this master plan of mine to him, his whole life flashing before or behind his eyes, wherever whole lives do their flashing. Rik was looking at him imploringly, and he was aware of it. 'Go through the lines, remind yourself of the moves onstage in front of an audience,' I said masterfully (after all, I wasn't the one who was going to have to do it, which was where my mastery of manner came from – though I was going to have to watch him do it, an ordeal at first remove). 'It'll be a small house, we'll treat it as a dress rehearsal.' The use of 'we' was a clear impertinence, but, ever the gentleman, Simon let it pass. Actually, I felt that I resembled one of those Great War generals of legend, who sent young soldiers over the tops of the trenches to their doom, while themselves remaining behind in a comfortably furnished dug-out or well behind the lines, with their port and Harrods hampers. I didn't have a Harrods hamper, though of course I had Stephen's first-night gift, the Fortnum and Mason's hamper, still unopened and, in the light of current events, somehow unopenable. But I did have my dug-out, behind the lines, in the form of Cell Block C, to which I could always retreat when the going got rough for Simon.

After only two days of proper rehearsal and without any chance to practise his costume changes or experience his lighting and sound cues, etc. (he'd have to have a little technical run at all that stuff in the morning), Simon was consigned to his manifest destiny: to go into the next day's matinée, manifestly under-prepared, knowing – as Rik and I did – that something was bound to go wrong anyway. Because something always goes wrong, even if you're over-prepared, as Stephen had been.

What went wrong was a very minor matter in one respect – two words were dropped from the last scene of Act One, and replaced by two words from the first scene of Act Two. On the other hand, they were two very important words. The first act scene leads up to – has its emotional climax in – Blake telling Bourke that the KGB intends him to stay in Moscow not for the week or so that Bourke had planned but for six months. In the second-act scene Blake informs Bourke that his sentence has been extended to five years, and that is the emotional climax of that scene. So Simon's minor slip, substituting 'five years' for 'six months' in the last scene in Act One, would completely invalidate the course of most of the first scene in Act Two. That so small a mistake, so trifling a matter as two wrong words – no, two right words in the wrong place – could be so disastrous, I thought, as I lurched back to Cell Block C, gulped down a glass of champagne, sucked some nicotine into myself to no calming effect whatsoever. Well, I was the author, I was the director, it was up to me to come up with something that would retrieve the situation. What I came up with was sheer nonsense – something along the lines of Blake's saying in the subsequent scene, 'Not five years. No. For the rest of your life.' That was the best I could do, and as I've said, it was nonsense. But at least it was logical, linear nonsense. I hurried out of the theatre as the curtain came down on the act, and caught Simon and Rik on their way to the dressing rooms. We stood looking at each other, the three of us, and simultaneously exploded into laughter. Helpless, clutching-at-each-other laughter. Re-realizing the urgency of the situation, I pulled myself together. 'Right,' I said, 'we've got a crisis here, let's face it. But what I think we do' – that 'we' again – 'is that in the next scene Simon says something to the effect that you've got to stay for the rest of your life. What do you think?' Rik and Simon looked at each other, bewildered. 'Why?' one of them said. 'Because we've got a crisis, we're running out of time, we've got to resolve it in some way or –' Rik and Simon stared at me as if I were slightly mad, which made them, from my point of view, completely mad.'There isn't a crisis,' Simon said, 'because Rik's already resolved it.' And he had. While I was working out my nonsensical solution in Cell Block C, then hurrying around the theatre to proffer it back-stage, Rik, on stage with Simon, having received the news of the five years' detention (that should have been six months) whispered, 'Tell me you're only joking.' 'I'm only joking,' Simon then said. 'It's not five years. It's only six months.' Which actually added an extra twist to Blake's cunning as bad-news-breaker – first inducing panic, then inducing relief, so that for Bourke the six months came as a kind of pardon. Rik, of course, had responded appropriately. So all 'we' had to do, when the five years came up (and it was coming up in about fifteen minutes' time), was to have Simon say sorrowfully, when he announced the five further years, 'And I'm afraid I'm not joking this time.' It worked so well – complicating Blake's deviousness by suggesting that his jokes were truths and therefore his truths might be jokes – that I was tempted to keep it in. But I didn't – out of superstition, I suppose, the feeling that an error corrected into a gain by accident would bring ill luck, the fates wouldn't tolerate it. Actually it wasn't really corrected by accident. It was corrected by Rik's quick-wittedness and Simon's quick-witted reaction to it.

I went back-stage after the show, for further merriment with the cast, and then on to the Ivy, to wait for Victoria and the evening performance of *Cell Mates*. I felt very trembly – no, was actually trembling slightly, as if from flu, or old age, or the exhaustion of the last few months, with virtually yet another first night to get through. And possibly trembling with the hope that at last the end was in sight – though, as it turned out, the end that was in sight was not the one I was looking towards. When Victoria arrived we sat on for a bit – she enjoyed all the six months/five years stuff, I heard about her day, and then we walked up to the Albery, I leaning on her as if she were a nurse to the elderly, my gait a bit of a shuffle, as if we were heading to a 'home' or a hospice, and not to a theatre, where I had a play on that I could boast was now having vastly more exposure and yet playing to much smaller houses than any other play in the West End.

The usual suspects, i.e. Duncan and Peter Wilkins, had rounded themselves up in Cell Block C. I felt too fragile to take them in properly, talk to them at all. I have a recollection that it was then – but it may have been on the occasion when he looked in on the understudy – that Duncan reported overhearing a middle-aged man saying to his middle-aged female companion (his wife, one trusts), 'Oh, *Cell Mates*. Yes. That's the play that's so awful Stephen Fry had to walk out on it.' Or words to that effect. Duncan, by the way, had moved the incomparable David Bownes to his (Duncan's) theatrical fiefdom in Chichester against my strongly expressed objections – Rik, the whole company, needs his attentiveness, his experienced understanding of their needs, I argued – but to no avail. David Bownes would be off to Chichester, pausing only to have a check-up for the ulcer that was his inevitable reward for all his gentle decency and consideration. I'd found this transfer of David Bownes distinctly ominous. Once a company manager is installed, he stays with the show until it ends, was my own experience. Until it ends. Were we ending, just as we were making our fresh start? It was a possible interpretation of his departure – that he was no longer needed at the Albery because shortly there would be nothing there to need him for. The new company manager was also a David, David Grant. Simon knew him well from other productions, and the rest of the cast took to him instantly.

After the show I went back-stage, went into Rik's dressing room, stood looking at him. He stood looking at me, half-dressed, a drink in his hand. 'What's the matter?' he said. 'Wasn't it all right? Wasn't I all right?' I burst into tears. I hadn't known I was going to, so that even in my crying I was as shocked as Rik. But he was only briefly shocked. He took me in his arms and kind of rocked me, swaying me about, murmuring gently, 'But I didn't know you cried, you're the one who never cries, but you cry now, you cry' – his tenderness made me cry more, of course. I imagine I was having a mini-breakdown, but it was his face that had done it, so beseechingly enquiring whether it was all right, whether he was all right – this man who'd worked so devotedly with the 'Stevie' he thought he knew and knew he loved, who had given himself over with such passionate completeness to Sean Bourke that he sometimes referred to himself, without thinking, as Sean, who had been betrayed every night on stage by Stephen's Blake, and then betrayed by Stephen himself, who'd acted with an understudy for ten performances while in emotional shock – had asked me whether 'it was all right', whether 'he was all right' – that's what did the trick, that's what tipped me over. So there I stood, blubbering, until I could bear no more of my helplessness, of Rik's tenderness, and went to the sofa and sat down. Rik poured me a Scotch, finished dressing; I composed myself and we went into Simon's dressing room where the company had assembled for notes. I gave them some, pretending to consult a pad on which there were indecipherable scrawlings, but I remembered quite a few things I hadn't noticed myself noticing, and it seemed important to behave as if this were just another moment in our professional lives – work went on.

I came out of Simon's dressing room. I found Duncan and Peter Wilkins hanging about in the corridor, waiting to visit the actors. 'We were just saying what a great job you've done, Stephen,' Duncan slurred, not drunk of course, though only drunk would have justified it. I let it pass. After all, he now had two Simons to deal with, and an absent Stephen, who must have been continually in his thoughts – to the extent, possibly, of his believing he had two or more Stephens and no Simons whatsoever. On the other hand it must have been a relief to discover that the two understudies, one of whom had had to stand in for Rik in Richmond, the other for Stephen at the Albery, were both called Michael, and that the company managers were both called David. And what did he call Raquel Welch? Perhaps her gender made him more attentive to her actual identity. Anyway, I let the confusion pass, what did it matter really whether I was writer/director Stephen, actor Simon, or living a darkly gastronomic life in Bruges as Monsieur Simon or whatever? And who am I to challenge Duncan on the misapplicatioan of names now that I suddenly remember that the two understudies were not Michael and Michael but Michael and Mark.

I left Duncan and Peter Wilkins – they were looking oddly forlorn, like bookies who'd taken a terrible beating from a three-legged horse – and went up to the Ivy, to join Victoria and Judy for the company dinner.

I don't remember much about the occasion, except that there was a great deal of hilarity, which Sam Dastor briefly dispelled by commenting on the smallness of the house – I have the impression that he did a finger-count, though I'm sure he didn't.

I went in on Thursday to do some rapid rehearsing, late in the afternoon but well before the half, then went down to the Ivy for a private drink, a lot of smoking, then dragged myself up to the evening performance. Another poor house, but a whistling, stamping, shouting one, all warmth and appreciation for Rik,

Simon and the stalwart, focused company that surrounded them. I went back-stage, ushered Simon into Rik's dressing room, and discussed their performances, about which I was deeply stupid and insensitive. My main note was for Rik, that he'd been forcing the pace, that Simon was at this stage – his third performance only, after all – still finding his way, having to take his time to feel for the right details in his Blake. The consequence was that the show had been two-paced, impetuous speediness from Rik, measured thoughtfulness from Simon – in other words, don't be impatient, Rik, Simon will catch up with you. Rik looked stricken, not surprisingly, as he'd just been struck, and by a man he'd soothed, the previous evening, through an emotional breakdown. The wiser course would have been to have spoken to Rik on his own; the wisest, to have said nothing at all, to have let them develop together, find their own rhythms as they lived together on stage. Really I seemed to be implying, I suppose, that Rik had bullied Simon through the play, which was not what I meant – I meant exactly what I should, as I've said, have left unsaid. I couldn't think of any way of unsaying it, apart from blustering on into compliments.

We went into Simon's dressing room, where the rest of the cast was waiting. I floundered through some notes, conscious that Rik was sitting crouched, in a haunted gloom. When I'd finished, he got up and left the room, burst, in fact, out of the room. Paul, Carole, Sam drifted off. I hung about Simon for a while, had a drink with him, then looked in on Rik.

He was manically cheerful, no doubt, on the humiliation I'd dished out to him. I made a tentative apology, and even as I was making it, I realized that enough was enough, anyway for the time being. Too much in us was raw, and from the same experience, the same shock. He brushed my apology aside, saying, no, no, I'd been right, he felt terrific, elated, he was going to cross the road to the pub, did I want to come? No, I said, I was going up to the Ivy to meet Victoria, did he want to come? No, he said, he wanted the atmosphere of the pub, the Irish atmosphere, Sean's sort of pub, so we agreed to go our separate ways. I then said, 'Look, I think I should leave the show alone for a while. Let you and Stephen –' doing a perfect Duncanism at the perfectly inappropriate time – 'Simon, I mean, Christ!, you and *Simon* get on with it.' So we parted, he to his Irish pub; I, suppressing a Judas-like feeling, to the Ivy. I told Victoria that I wasn't going into the theatre for a bit, then gave her a faltering account of my apprehensions that the show was doomed, that it would close soon, there was something going on, I said, something apart from the falling houses, that Rik and I didn't know about but had got into our system. Something not quite right. She was unbelieving, no doubt suspecting the usual paranoia.

We were off to Barbados on the following Saturday. I decided my next trip to the Albery would be on Thursday, by which time Simon and Rik would have settled in completely, and I myself might have settled down. Settling down was difficult. I footled about in my study with Sarah, dealing with long-unanswered correspondence, signed cheques with a dubious future, made jokes to Sarah about the dubious future of *Cell Mates*, to which she responded as Victoria responded; talked frequently on the phone to Judy, who said, when I put it to her that I was worried about Duncan's intentions, that he'd given out no negative hints, that theatres were pretty empty at the moment all over London, we were doing no worse than a lot of plays, though we'd probably be doing a lot better than all of them if Stephen hadn't defected. No, she said, she couldn't see why he'd close it – after all, he'd gone ahead with Simon, hadn't he?

To me, Stephen had become a kind of ogre. Absent, invisible, he was to be seen every day in the press, on television, reported on for not being there to report on.

> As I was going down the stair
> I met a man who wasn't there –
> He wasn't there again today
> I wish to God he'd go away.

Although I was still angry with Stephen, I never, have never, wished him harm. But during the days before my next visit to the theatre, I found myself shooting one of his poster-selfs through the throat with the cap gun Rik had given me on the first night, making the same noise before I fired that Stephen used to make as Blake – a long hiss – - hiss, bang, I went through Stephen's throat. But it didn't do any good. I couldn't blast his highly visible invisible self out of the limelight, however many caps I slayed him with.

And I couldn't get Rik to blast himself into the limelight, where he belonged. But there we had it. Stephen, absent, was publicly everywhere, which he must have hated more than anyone else; while Rik, present on the stage, refused to be present anywhere else. He turned down all opportunities – and they were numerous, they were clamouring – to be interviewed, not even on a highly popular show whose host was a fan of Rik's, had been to the show and admired it, and promised to concentrate only on the play, Rik and Simon Ward. I talked to and faxed Rik's agent, Aude Powell, who understood how important positive publicity would be to the survival of *Cell Mates*. She equally understood the source of Rik's reticence, his need to let what was on stage speak for itself. And there had been an unpleasant publicity gaffe. On the day on or after Rik had received Stephen's letter announcing his departure, he'd had to honour an engagement to appear on *Pebble Mill*, the BBC television chat show which is done live in Birmingham. He wanted to cancel, but it was too late. So down he had to go, to Birmingham, knowing – as the people on the programme did not – that Stephen had vanished. He was asked, in enthusiastic innocence, what sort of time he and Stephen were having together, what was it like to work with an old friend, etc. Rik had no idea what to say. All that he knew was that he couldn't, yet, tell the truth. The experience must have been a nightmare, really – particularly at its climax when, invited by the interviewer to sing a few lines from 'Danny Boy', the song that Rik sings periodically throughout the play, Rik forgot the words. Forgot the words. A song he'd been singing for weeks and weeks, and he couldn't remember the words. After which he came back to London, to the Albery and Stephen's understudy, where he sang 'Danny Boy' perfectly. Well, perfectly in terms of the play, which was all that was required. But he knew all the words of course.

Rik moved backwards and forwards, from grief to rage to grief – the only time he felt free from his inner turmoil was when he could be Sean, 'his Sean', on stage.

But otherwise he was to himself a loose cannon. Or loose cap gun, as it was to turn out. Unlike myself, who was a disciplined cap gun, shooting at posters and not even scaring the two cats – one fat and grey called Harry, although a female, sexually misdi-agnosed at birth, and the other a mainly black, with white paws, less fat, but fat nonetheless female, called Tom, also sexually misdiagnosed at birth. Neither cat quivered in the slightest on passing through my windows to the garden below as I fired away at Stephen's neck.

Simon Ward, however, that dutiful but on this occasion so far unscarred (except by *The Times*) soldier, was fighting on every front. He rose at six one morning to write a fleet-footed article for the *Telegraph* on what it was like to take over in such excep-tional, indeed unique, circumstances. Went on to do a series of interviews all over London, perhaps even out of London, and then turned up on the stage to give his performance – growing in subtlety, the stage manager informed me – every night. 'Pity,' he added, 'that there were so few to enjoy it.'

Monday, Tuesday, Wednesday passed meaninglessly, as I hadn't sprung myself emotionally from *Cell Mates*. On Thursday, two days before the flight to Barbados, I was back in Cell Block C, and then in the auditorium, watching the perfor-mance. David Grant was right, it had grown – grown out of all proportion to the audience, although that too was showing signs of growth. Victoria came with me but I don't remember any-body else being there – a kind of private viewing is what it seemed like.

When I went back-stage, Rik pulled me into his dressing room, smiling and intense, asking what I thought, how had they progressed, he and Simon? He was, as on my last visit, in manic and needy mode. 'Why don't you come and have dinner at the

Ivy,' I said, 'with Simon and Alexandra?' 'No,' he said. 'No, I want to go home. We'll get them back,' he said. 'The punters. We'll get them in. The bums back on the seats.' I began to say that the way to get the punters to put their bums on the seats would be by having him remind them that the show was still on, that he was still in it, but refrained. Because I suddenly realized there was pride at stake here. In a taxi once he'd told me that he'd been successful for many years, since his early twenties he'd managed to fill theatre after theatre, he could fill the largest theatre in the country all on his own, it was axiomatic, automatic really. And now here he was in the West End in by no means the largest theatre in the country, and there were precious few punters putting their bums where they ought to be. But the truth of the matter was that very few people knew he was still at the Albery, and millions upon millions knew that Stephen Fry, currently a media megastar, had left the Albery for Bruges, or an anonymous life as a prep-school teacher, according to one of the recent announcements, or a life as a teacher of English, its language and – presumably – its values, according to another, and nothing Rik could do, apart from appearing on television chat shows, giving interviews, could alter the situation – that he was rendered anonymous by Stephen's aspiration to anonymity. So it was pride in his name, deservedly earned, and pride in his performance, deservedly acclaimed, along with an inability to speak out his feelings about Stephen, that kept Rik and *Cell Mates* out of public attention. But, as I say, I didn't say any of that. What would have been the use? One thing Rik and Stephen have in common is that they are both famous, and, unlike me, they both have their pride – and I wasn't prepared to show my own lack of pride by begging Rik to promote *Cell Mates*, just as I wouldn't have dreamt of showing it to Stephen earlier, by flying to Bruges – I'm sure I'd have spotted him in a jiffy, with or without his beret, putting my hand on his shoulder and saying, 'You are Stephen Fry and I claim your immediate return to the Albery Theatre.'

So I had to settle for Rik's insistence that we would get them back, the punters and their bums, we'd win through. He gave me a fierce, combative hug, and told me to have a good time in Barbados. But there was a gleam in his eye, a hint of desperation, that made me edgy on his behalf.

We had a jolly time at the Ivy, much laughter, many compliments from me to Simon; he said how much he admired Rik on stage, enjoyed his company off stage, and so it flowed. Towards the end of the meal Victoria suddenly spotted Duncan on the far side of the restaurant, sitting with a very elegant-looking lady whom I couldn't see properly, but took on faith to be a star.

On the way out we stopped by Duncan's table. He introduced me to his lady companion who was indeed famous, a very famous star, a very famous American star, to whom he'd introduced me once or twice before over the years. I said, bluntly but quite gently, I believe, that I hadn't seen or heard from him recently. 'Well,' he said, his eyes suddenly becoming highly inactive, fixing themselves with deliberate dullness over one of my shoulders, 'you seem to be managing fine on your own. I hear it's going very well. And that you're –' this to Simon – 'doing a great job on the publicity front.' Simon reeled off a list of his commitments the next day, which seemed to begin with a breakfast something or other at an hour in the morning I've never been around at, and then on to this interview, on to that interview, virtually finishing just in time to go on stage. I said that Victoria and I were off on holiday – looking at my watch and seeing that it was well after midnight – tomorrow. We exchanged a few brief pleasantries with his very famous American star, then left.

There was something about the conversation with Duncan that intensified my fears for the future of Cell Mates. It was nothing actually said, Duncan's sentences had all been compliments, studded with words like 'good' and 'great' and 'fine job' and wishes for a wonderful holiday. Perhaps it was simply that in his introductions and exchanges he'd got every single name right. For some reason this suggested to me that his mind was ominously focused on an elsewhere. I struggled to remember whether he'd said 'God bless'. But I couldn't work out whether I hoped he had or hoped he hadn't.

The next day was spent doing the kind of clearing up that's needed when preparing for a holiday. The only swimming trunks I could find were elderly, with a slightly tattered look to them. Victoria went shopping and came back with two pairs, both of which I liked. I paid off a number of bills with Sarah, who left in the early evening, I phoned Judy to say goodbye, see you in a week, lots of love. We began to pack. The plane left early in the morning – if we got it all done immediately we could have a leisurely dinner.

Judy rang again, half an hour after our last conversation. I knew from her tone exactly what she was going to say, which she then said: Duncan had decided to close the show, he was having the notice posted tomorrow, the show would be dead in two Saturdays' time. She asked me not to tell anyone in the company for the moment until Aude Powell, Rik's agent, had had a chance to break the news to Rik, she hadn't managed to locate him, he'd been out and about with his family somewhere. I thought of Rik probably heading towards the theatre as Judy and I spoke, sinking himself back into the part on the way there, lying down on the sofa to concentrate on his beloved Sean; and of Simon, on his way back from the last of his many interviews to promote the play; of the other innocents in the cast, Paul, Carole, Sam, putting on their make-up for their first scenes, anticipating a decent house, this being a Friday, going over a few of their lines. I said, no, I wouldn't tell anyone. 'I'm sorry,' Judy said. 'So very sorry.' Not meaning any irony in echoing Stephen's exit lines.

So there it was. *Cell Mates* was pronounced to be on its deathbed and would in two weeks' time be buried in the theatre's equivalent of a paupers' graveyard. It had no future in any other venue, in Britain or abroad, that I could see, no chance of resurrection, it had died of a fatal contamination, of a sequence, each leading into the other, of fatal contaminations. It had been murdered. No, that wasn't the word. *Cell Mates* had been killed by an act of collective manslaughter.

I said all this to Victoria, in a calm, fevered state. Over dinner I berated the fates for dumping on me this hideous combination of garbages. Five years of writing, three and a half months of directing, a success more than in the offing, and out of all this a disaster – I went on and on and on, my voice, I suspect, a dreary monotone of misery, incredulity, and belief.

We left the restaurant with only one decision made. That, as we were packed, I'd organize a taxi for the airport the next morning, which we'd probably cancel when it arrived. A cornucopia of options. We set the alarm for the earliest hour – far too early, incomprehensibly early for me – and at the last minute we'd do whatever – whatever ...

In the morning we lay in bed debating – to go or not to go? My suddenly being firm in my decision that I had to stay (partly because I didn't want to get up), Victoria suddenly and firmly indecisive, worried about the company, worried about the wasted funds if we didn't go, worried about my health, worried about how I would feel about the abandonment – but what can I do? I kept saying, it's over, though still hoping to hang about in bed, in the name of duty. It was far too early to call Rik and Simon. They'd either have not received the news or had had a late night, probably both; it wouldn't be right to disturb them, and what was there to say if they had received the news? There was nothing I could do. We either clambered ourselves into the taxi and went to the airport, or stayed behind to nurse the actors through the dying of the play. I veered strongly towards the position that we should stay. So did Victoria. Until we found ourselves out of bed, getting clothed, dragging our bags into the taxi and heading for the airport. In the taxi we talked of heading back, at the airport we talked of heading back, in the plane we stopped talking, she being in an aisle seat non-smoker, I being in an aisle seat smoker. I picked up a morning newspaper in which Stephen featured prominently – this may have been the tabloid in which he was reported as being spotted in Eastern Europe. Where was he heading? To Moscow, with the intention of ending up in a flat shared with a Blake who'd be played by himself? I discarded the tabloid, and lowered my head inertly over a ponderously written thriller. We were on our way to Barbados, with its powerfully balming sun, its tranquil sea, whether we liked it or not.

PART VI

What we arrived at is where I began this chronicle. Howling winds, followed the next day by howling winds, with no-swimming red flags out, followed by torrential rains, followed by the theft of my two newly acquired pairs of swimming trunks, along with my duty-free Silk Cut and my lighter. There I sat, in my old and tattered swimming trunks, a half-nude tramp, still struggling (why?) to read the dud thriller I'd failed to read on the plane. Once, I remember, I made a positive attempt to face up to the brute facts of my situation, but the best I could manage was to peer at them, with my hand over my eyes, through the gaps between my fingers. Putting aside the double irony of being on a holiday that had so far provided only the opportunity for bodily mortification and was, furthermore, as I believe I've already mentioned, a holiday I could afford neither to be on, nor (given the kind of sum I'd have lost in losing my deposit) *not* to be on – putting aside this comparatively trivial if paradoxical disaster, there lay ahead of me the full consequences of the untimely end of *Cell Mates*. Consequences which presented themselves in a sequence of such deadening words as 'bills', 'overdrafts', 'mortgages', 'responsibilities', 'dependants', and in such lively images as scissors flashing through credit cards, returned cheques bouncing jeeringly through the letter-box, grovelling encounters in rooms packed with creditors – and furthermore, or furtherless, I was nudging sixty. I sealed my fingers tightly over my eyes, preferring momentary darkness to the prospect of my future, my lack of a future. 'But good heavens,' I thought, 'good heavens,' lowering my hands and coming back into the light, 'what are they to do with the living spirit, these merely material concerns?' And my living spirit was surely being tended to – for what other purpose this buffeting by the winds, this drenching in the rain? Yes, everything would be all right as long as God was in His heaven. Which He clearly was. With a sudden moan from the living spirit, a moan, I trust, of profound contentment, I picked up my glass of champagne, now diluted and rendered lifeless by drops of rain and spray, picked up my still dud and now slightly soggy thriller, and crouched there, there in the bar, in a posture that from a distance must have resembled that of an ageing penitent, oblivious to the turbulence around him, doggedly at his devotions.

I got a phone call from Judy, to say that houses were picking up (so what?), but she was sorry to have to inform me, 'sorry to have to inform you' were her actual words, that Rik, after a performance, had rollicked crazily around Covent Garden, finally pulling one of his cap guns on an innocent couple, a middle-aged innocently strolling couple, American, she thought (and I hoped – who could be more worthy targets than middle-aged, almost certainly anti-smoking American tourists?) – and fired off some caps at them and, if not blowing them away, momentarily blew them back to New York and violent death. A couple of policemen saw him at it, or heard the Americans scream – whatever – and frogmarched Rik to a nearby station from which, after an hour or two of contrition and apologies, he was released. This a was painful story to hear. The Rik I knew could be boisterous company, but never violent, except in a comic turn, when the pretended violence induced laughter, not fear. This cap-gun episode was also, I suppose, intended to be a comic turn, but played out in the wrong context, an impulsive release of his frustration and anger, his (still unmassaged) grief at Stephen's betrayal. I felt guilty. Perhaps I should have been back-stage at the Albery after the show, with a beret on my head and a menu from Bruges in my pocket. Then Rik could have fired at me instead of roving around the West End, his cap gun in his pocket, his psyche itchy-fingered, trigger-happy.

A couple of days later, in one of the patches of brilliant sunshine, when I'd had confirmed by Judy that there had been no reprieve, the notice had been posted, the news would be on the front pages shortly, I sent a fax to the company expressing my admiration for their sense of duty (and sense of humour) in the line of fire. Then I took out one of the American yellow legal pads I'd brought with me in the hope that I'd be able to struggle through a new draft of a television script I'd put aside some years ago. Instead I began this account of my experiences with *Cell Mates*.

Now here I am back in London on Good Friday, with Rik's first-night gift of a cap gun to hand, Stephen's neck still available on a number of posters that still litter the room. As I write this, Stephen is no longer on the front pages, and haunts the inside pages only in asides. The big theatrical story at the moment is of Raquel Welch and the poor reception she's been getting for her performance in *The Millionairess* everywhere she goes – Guildford, Richmond and currently Birmingham. Fearing that she might not make it to London after all, the *Standard* splashed the news of her humiliation across its front page, and then hustled somebody down to Birmingham to review Ms Welch – unfavourably, of course – even though the long-established tradition is that shows travelling to, or attempting to travel to, a London theatre don't get reviewed by the nationals and the *Standard* (the London newspaper, after all) until they reach their destination. This struck me as a very nasty operation, unprecedented if there hadn't been so many recent precedents. I noted, of course, that though Ms Welch's failure had become the capital's hot news from the provinces, she continued to 'tread the boards' every night.

The weather in Barbados finally turned into Barbados weather and, as we'd had such short rations, we extended our holiday by a further two days, which would still get us back in time for the last night on Saturday. I spent half a day rearranging the plane tickets, and the next day, the full extra day, crouching where I'd come to believe I belonged, in the shelter of the bar, as the rain beat down, the winds howled, a kind of younger Lear with a yellow pad, but without the necessary words, as Shakespeare had used them up. The last day – we were to leave in the evening –

was tauntingly beautiful, the air fresh as well as warm, the sea almost transparent, with the prospect of many more days like this to follow. Or so we were informed by the waiters and the management – the waiters confiding that they actually preferred the windy days which kept them cooler in their uniforms, and the management not confiding what was obvious – that it preferred windy, rainy days, because the clientele huddled in the bar and bought far more drinks than on usual Barbadian days. On the other hand, both waiters and management needed the sun and the calm, the hopping birds, the cheerful sunny listlessness, to attract people to the island in the first place, or they would all be out of jobs. We had probably experienced, from their point of view, the perfect holiday: lots of money-making wind, rain, unswimmable-in seas, with enough sunny days to make us prolong our stay in the hope of more, then rain on the last full day, sun on what we had of the last day, a day that made us long to stay on longer, and certainly dream of coming back some year, as soon as possible, which for me turned it, from the financial aspect, into a never-never land. I couldn't see how I could afford to get there, let alone stay there.

The next evening we were back in Cell Block C, along with Judy and Aude, but no representative from the management. The house was almost full (papered?), with the actors giving the best performance I'd ever seen, taking leave of each other as characters, Bourke and Blake and Zinaida knowing they would never see each other again, Stan and Viktor watching Bourke's leave-taking with affection and melancholy. The audience responded emotionally, a noisy tribute to Rik and Simon, the whole company, a tribute and a farewell. When the final curtain fell there came an extraordinary howl from behind it, of joyful and angry defiance. A howl from Rik, of course.

Afterwards I went straight to Rik's dressing room. We stood looking at each other in a tangle of feelings that even now I can't begin to disentangle. He locked the door, poured us drinks, we held each other's cheeks in a helpless, eye-dribbling stillness, stroking each other's cheeks gently, but it was very still, no speech possible. I drank the drink, he unlocked the door to admit his friends and fans, I visited the other actors – Simon, cheerfully and professionally fatalistic, saying he couldn't come to Rik's party as his mother or mother-in-law, I forget which, had descended on a visit, and he had to get back to her. We embraced in the Russian mode, the mode of the two cell mates holed up in Moscow, agreed to speak on the phone in a day or so (which we did) to arrange a dinner (which I'm sure we'll have), then I looked in on Carole, Sam and Paul, who were all entertaining friends (ticket-paying ones, I hoped), thanked, hugged and – in Carole's case – kissed, and looked forward to meeting in an hour or so, *chez* Rik.

At the Ivy, Victoria, Judy and I had a quick meal, talked over this new lot of abruptly old times. We didn't stay long. Judy had brought her car, and drove us in it to Rik's house. A large house, a lot of large rooms, with an opulent family feel, worth standing up for, even as a stand-up comic. The people standing up in all this space were, besides members of the cast – minus Simon – the stage management and crew, and Rik's friends. Rik grabbed me by the arm and said, 'Let's go outside and talk.' He pulled me to the front steps, where we sat down. It was a composed conversation in comparison with the unspoken one we'd had only an hour or so before, untactile and almost matter-of-fact. He said he believed he'd learned a lot from what had happened with Stephen, had 'grown up' in some way. I said I hoped to God he'd come back from time to time to the legitimate theatre, he was the bee's knees – a great actor, and a valiant man, there was no point being the former if you weren't the latter, and he'd shown he was both. Neither of us mentioned our respective cap guns, my shooting Stephen through the poster neck, his caper with the Americans in Covent Garden. I'm sure he knew I knew about his behaviour. I wasn't sure he knew about mine. We talked a little bit about the possibility of our doing something else together some time, some time. We agreed to talk about it after he got back from Barbados. 'Barbados? Really? What hotel are you going to?' It was the same one we'd just come back from, though he hadn't known where we were staying. A coincidence.

One of his children, Sid it must have been, came through the door, flung himself across Rik, demanded to be carried back into the house. Rik carried him back. I sat for a while on the doorstep, facing up to the fact that these moments, the tranquil conversation with Rik, the solitary drink on the doorstep, the moments about to come – the last quick hugs with the rest of the cast – really meant the end of *Cell Mates*.

I don't know where Stephen is now. He came back to London from his hamlet and deposited himself briefly in a private hospital for treatment for something or other of a nervous nature. But I did hear from Judy, who got it from someone or other, probably Duncan or Peter Wilkins, that he stubbornly refused to be examined by the insurance company's doctor.

Why? After all, the act committed was the act committed, the manner of it was the manner of it. In his public utterance, and in his two letters to me, Stephen insisted upon accepting responsibility for the havoc he'd created. Possibly one day, and possibly quite soon, after he and Duncan and the insurance company have sorted out the financial problems between them, he will sidle back by way of a television confession, or a long interview with one of the newspapers. Then back to work, little by little, a guest appearance, a television spot, a chat show of his own, until the public defection of Stephen Fry will be an affectionately regarded, when remembered, incident in his biography. Or autobiography. Who knows? He may be actually in the private hospital still, sending out applications to teach in prep schools, state schools, public schools, language schools abroad. Who knows? Ms Raquel Welch in *The Millionairess* will be a joke, revived from time to time, but of no consequence. But whenever Stephen surfaces, whether with a public smile on television or in the most obscure teaching school in a remote corner of Europe, he will be in the limelight again, whether he wants it or not.

So, in spite of everything I've written so far about Stephen, I realize I still know nothing, or at least nothing conclusive, about him. But here are a few blundering speculations.

Stephen has been rich – perhaps even very rich – from a very young age. Which means that he can talk of money with contempt, which might also mean that he can be casually unimagining about other people's lack of it. Perhaps it never crossed his mind that as a consequence of his defection people he knew and trusted, people who knew, trusted and looked after him, would be thrown out of work, back on the dole, to their first homes, without a second, and professional, home to go to.

Then again, there's the question of his celibacy. Is it possible that celibates who publicly declare their celibacy *daren't* look other people in the eye, in case some glimmer of normal lust, the longing for human contact, shows itself? And by celibacy I don't mean just an abstinence from sexual contact, but a resolutely maintained distance from any form of emotional entanglement – *'noli me tangere'* in any part of myself, though I'll have lunch with you, or dinner with you, meet you at your favourite bar, one of my clubs, if I'm not too busy sharing myself with the television millions, always available but never there. Was this his initial problem in the scenes when he was alone with Rik, *'noli me tangere'*? Because with Rik it was almost the absolute opposite. Touch, hold, support – *help me!* And help me demonstratively, *feel* me – there was always an element of this in what Rik gave to and demanded from the audience; hopelessly and helplessly available, he needed to be taken. And most of us feel the same, the need to be taken and loved – 'Whose little boy are you?' Audiences reach out eagerly towards not just Rik but the character he's playing. And the knowledge that they're doing so gives him the courage to play the characters he plays. His need makes the characters larger, richer, than on the page. Well, that was certainly true of his Bourke. But *'noli me tangere'* gives you only the courage to be alone.

Or at the centre of a party.

No man who lives alone, who *chooses* to live alone, has the opportunity to be in continuous intelligent communication with himself – the conversation is likely to be either escalatingly monomaniacal (solipsistic) or despairingly schizophrenic. Well, that is my view – which is only the view of someone who hates the thought of living alone. So in my view – in my experience – a living, other partner argues, disagrees, lovingly or angrily points out that he or she is also there, that you are merely you, that one is only one – in other words, that a couple is more, far more, than just two. A partner of any kind – a true friend – i.e. someone Stephen could talk to – would have ridiculed his response to his bad reviews, and had him laughing at them and at himself. They would not have allowed to say, 'Sorry. Very sorry' into an answering machine before letting him hike off – without speaking to his sister, his parents, any of the friends he entertained at Christmas, Rik, or me even – to Bruges where he managed to be, however unwillingly, the centre of a party thrown by television and the press. Pascal said something along these lines: that all human evil came from men not being able to stay alone in a room. He didn't go on to consider the effects of a man innerly alone and outwardly gregarious in a room full of people dependent on him.

Sometimes when I'm in a small, secure swimming pool, splashing reluctantly about in it because the red flags are up on the beach and the sea is unavailable, I'm overcome by a terror of sharks – that there's one in the water with me, moving with mechanical purpose towards a foot, an arm. Water, even in small amounts, is an irrational place – or rather, can be the cause of irrationality. But so can small areas of dry land, like the Albery Theatre in London. Stephen, after the *Financial Times* review, might have had the same terror of the stage that I've had of the water in swimming pools. There are no sharks in swimming pools, I announce pedantically to myself, as I thrash urgently towards the nearest steps. Reviews can't hurt me, Stephen reminds himself, as he thrashes his way towards Bruges.

It was surely hell in Bruges for Stephen, clutching his English newspapers; hell in Eastern Europe, clutching or searching for his English newspapers; hell in the South of France, in the hamlet where there were probably no English newspapers at all, and so found himself besieged by imaginary headlines. I would rather have been Rik at the Albery, Simon Ward coming into and almost immediately out of the Albery, the company thrown out of work, the stage management made redundant, than Stephen in Bruges. Eastern Europe. The South of France. He wasn't simply a wilful outcast, but an outcast who'd messed up the lives of others, and each piece of news must have been a torment. Especially the news that his long press statement, honourably issued, honestly expressed, that was an attempt to save the production and Rik's future in it, had backfired, not against himself but against the production and Rik, thus neatly reversing T. S. Eliot's famous line – Stephen had done the wrong thing for the right reason. As I had done in my press release. Above all we needed his silence. As we did mine. If only -

The problem with 'if onlys' is that they aren't expressed on a single occasion, or now and then. One continues to inflame oneself with them to no purpose, while boring others. 'I spent five years of my life working in some capacity or other on *Cell Mates*,' I say to myself and others, 'and if only Stephen Fry –' I flinch as I hear myself saying it, and try to find a more philosophical tone, or, even better, a different subject. Images come back to me, from cheerful days of rehearsals at the Old Vic, of Stephen's laughter as he and Rik shared one of their extraordinary flights of ingenuous fantasy, gambolling about the rehearsal room as if it were a play-pen; of Sam always slightly too visible and too noisy as he flicked over the pages of his script, learning his lines; of Paul, always slightly too invisible, beaming shy apologies as he arrived only to the second, or sometimes the second after it, for the day's work; of Carole, omnipresent but never intrusive, padding up to play the Russian housekeeper, converting her naturally graceful walk into a slow, stamping waddle. Those were certainly happy days, as happy if not happier than any I've ever experienced in the theatre, in spite of the constant knot of tension in my stomach. And then on to Guildford and Richmond, the note-givings followed by little parties in the dressing rooms. There was so much merriment, that was it, so much *merriment* – until the tears in Rik's dressing room. So the 'if onlys' come back relentlessly, the memories of happiness and merriment inducing misery and rancour. A final image, delivered as if by the gloating gods, of the front of house after the last night, as I was heading towards the Ivy. There they all were, the quotes I'd begged for from the management, all of them up at last, including one for Simon Ward extracted from Stephen's press release – it would have made for any playwright/director a gratifying view, especially if he were passing it on his way to celebration. But no, there's a final, final image on my way to the splendours of the front of house. On the walls there were still small-scale posters of Rik and Stephen, separated by prison bars, large-scale versions of which I still have curled on the shelves behind me, *memento mori* that I can't bring myself to touch, though I long to tear them up.

Just after I'd written these words, Stephen was back in the newspapers, sighted at Heathrow Airport as he was about to board a plane to Los Angeles. To do what? Who knows? When asked by a journalist how he was feeling, he apparently replied, 'A bit better now, thank you.'

As I was going down the stair –

My fate. To have met a man who wasn't there. A man who, like his producer, ended almost all his farewells with a 'God Bless'. But perhaps fate is too grandiose a word to explain it all. Chance might be the proper word.

But then, however often I go down the stair, up and down the stair, will I again chance upon an actor with the gifts of Rik Mayall, the man who, for all his anxieties and vulnerabilities, was always there? Slim chance, I think. Slimmest of chances.